Challenge & Change

A World Study after 1900

PHILIP INGRAM

Hodder & Stoughton

A MEMBER OF THE HODDER HEADLINE GROUP

Acknowledgements

For Susan

The front cover shows Nelson Mandela reproduced courtesy of Camera Press/ H Lindgren, and celebrations on top of the Berlin Wall on 10 November 1989, reproduced courtesy of Associated Press, Berlin.

The publishers would like to thank the following individuals, institutions and companies for permission to reproduce copyright illustrations in this book:
AKG, p2(Le Petit Journal, 13th May 1906 'Les Manifestations du 1 Mai a Paris'), pp 68, 69; AKG/Erich Lessing, p 34bl(Morning of the Motherland, by Fyodor Schurpin, 1949); AKG/John Heartfield © DACS, 2000 ('The Meaning of the Hitler Salute – millions are behind me', AIZ Magazine cover, vol. 11, no. 42, 16th Oct l932), p37tr; Amalgamated Engineering & Electrical Union (AEEU), Esher, p45b; Anti-Slavery International, p3t/93t(NNRU LN HKJI); Associated Press, pp84t, 85tl; Associated Press/Jean-Marc Bouju, p73; Associated Press/Topham, p90l; Associated Press/Greg Marinovitch, p82b; Bildarchiv Osterreichische Nationalbibliothek, p12t(155.P74/BR), p12b (RV 35PO/B); Bildarchiv Preussischer Kulturbesitz, p38t(F14095)&b(F4898), p40c(F8437); Bilderdienst Suddeutscher Verlag, p36; Bodleian Library, University of Oxford: John Johnson collection: Electricity and Electrical Applicances 3, p46t; Bundesarchiv, Koblenz, p40l(poster for the film The Eternal Jew); Camera Press, p88t&b, Camera Press/Jonathan Haddock, p89, Camera Press/Robbie King, p82t; Corbis/Baci, p93b; Corbis/Bettmann, pp49t&b, 84bl, 85br; Corbis/Leif Skoogfors, p92tr; Corbis/Peter Turnley, p74r; Corbis/Nazima Kowall, p81r; Corbis/Underwood & Underwood, p46b; Chicago Historical Society, p48b(neg ICHi-30046 (detail), photographer Jun Fujita; David King Collection, pp 29t&b, 30l&c(stills from Eisenstein's film October, 1927), 32, 34t&bl, p35(Memorable Occasion, 1936), 53b, p78b(Krokodil, Issue no 2, 1952); D.C. Thomson & Co Ltd/ 'Commando' war stories, p54; Dod Miller/Network Photographers, p91b; Harris/© Times Newspapers Ltd, p80l(The Times, front page 18.1.99); H-Burkard/ Bilderberg/ Network Photographers, p90r; Hulton Getty, pp4t, 10, 25, 44t&b, 45t, 50/92, 51, 56b, 57b, 70, 71, 85bl; Imperial War Museum p14b(Q33128), p14l, p14r(Q 33161), p15t(POS 327), p15(Q 70864), p17t&b, p18, p19(MH 30895), p20Q11586), p21(3539, neg POS70), p24t(2722 neg Q80362), p24b(Q55013), p 37tl(HU51084), p39(HU7612), p40r(MH11470), p41(2564), p56t(HU44272), p60t(3188); Library of Congress, Washington, p47(LC-USZC4-6032), p48t/92tl(LC-USZC-4-2426); London Fire Brigade, p57t; Magyar Nemzeti Galeria, Budapest/ Bridgeman Art Library, Stalin in the Kremlin by Fedor Pavlovic Resetnikov (1906-83), Magyar Nemzeti Galeria, Budapest/ Bridgeman Art Library © State Tretyakov Gallery, Moscow, p60b; Marianna Belova © DACS/RAO, Moscow, 1999, Stalin as War Leader by Petr Lekseevich Belov, 1980s, ©DACS 2000, p61; Mary Evans/Fawcett Library pp4b, 5; National Army Museum, London, courtesy of the Director, p 7; Nguyen Kong/Associated Press, p84bl; Novosti (London), p 59t; Peter Newark's Military Pictures, p 11(The Canadians at Ypres by W.B. Wollen, 1915), p 53t, p 65(front page of Collier's Magazine, Dec 12, 1942, by Arthur Szyk); PA News/David Jones, p81l; PA News/Tony Harris, p92b; Popperfoto, p75tr; Popperfoto/Reuters, p74l(Source: International Defence & Aid Fund for South Africa), pp 75t, 80r, 91tl&tr; Ronald Grant Archive, p6(still from Ghandi, 1982), p30br(still from Eisenstein's film October, 1927), Ronald Grant Archive & David James © 1998 TM & Dreamworks, p 62(still from Saving Private Ryan, 1998); Solo Syndication Ltd p 6r; The Museum of London, p 3b(CL99/3832, The Bayswater Omnibus by G.W. Joy, 1895); TRH/Robert Hunt Library, p58t, 59b; Ullstein Bilderdienst, p42; United Nations, p83.

(key: r right; l left; t top; c centre; b below)

We are unable to trace the following and would be grateful for any information that would enable us to do so, p 33, 66, 75b, 79.

Picture research by Rebecca Teevan.

The publishers would also like to thank the following for permission to reproduce material in this book:
Extracts from Timewatch in 1988 reproduced with permission of BBC Licensing; The extract from Out of the Doll's House by Angela Holdsworth reprinted on page 50 is reproduced with the permission of BBC Worldwide Limited. Copyright © Angela Holdsworth 1988; Truman by Roy Jenkins, HarperCollins, 1986 reproduced by permission of Lord Jenkins; Ten Days that Shook the World by John Reed, Lawrence & Wishart, London 1961 (first published in England by the Communist Party of Great Britain, 1926), reproduced by permission of Lawrence & Wishart; Total War: The Causes and Courses of the Second World War by Peter Calvocoressi, Guy Wint and John Pritchard (Allen Lane, the Penguin Press, 1972, Revised edition 1989) copyright © Peter Calvocoressi, 1972, 1989, reproduced by permission of Penguin Books Ltd; Death's Men: Soldiers of the Great War by Dennis Winter (Allen Lane, 1978) copyright © Dennis Winter, 1978, reproduced by permission of Penguin Books Ltd; The First Day of the Somme: 1 July 1916 by Martin Middlebrook (Penguin Books, 1984) copyright © Martin Middlebrook, 1984, reproduced by permission of Penguin Books Ltd; A Century of Women: A History of Women in Britain and the United States by Sheila Rowbotham (Penguin Books, 1997) copyright © Sheila Rowbotham, 1997, reproduced by permission of Penguin Books Ltd; Sutton Publishing Limited for the extract from Women in the 1920's by Pamela Horn, Sutton Publishing Ltd, 1995; The Informed Heart by B Bettelhelm, Thames and Hudson Ltd, 1960, reproduced by permission of Thames & Hudson Ltd; From The Great War by Jay Winter and Blaine Baggett, copyright © 1996 by Community Television of Southern California. Used by permission of Penguin, a division of Penguin Putnam Inc.; Purnell's History of the 20th Century, Macdonald Young Books Ltd reproduced with permission of Wayland Publishers.

Please note that some sources have been adapted to make them more accessible to students.

Every effort has been made to trace and acknowledge ownership of copyright. The publishers will be glad to make suitable arrangements with any copyright holders whom it has not been possible to contact.

Orders: please contact Bookpoint Ltd, 130 Milton Park, Abingdon, Oxon OX14 4SB. Telephone: (44) 01235 827720, Fax: (44) 01235 400454. Lines are open from 9.00 - 6.00, Monday to Saturday, with a 24 hour message answering service. Email address: orders@bookpoint.co.uk

British Library Cataloguing in Publication Data
A catalogue record for this title is available from The British Library

ISBN 0 340 74233 X

First published 2000
Impression number 10 9 8 7 6 5 4 3
Year   2005 2004 2003 2002 2001

Typeset by Liz Rowe.
Printed in Italy for Hodder & Stoughton Educational, a division of Hodder Headline Plc, 338 Euston Road, London NW1 3BH by Printer Trento, Italy.

Contents

THE BIG PICTURE

THIS CHAPTER ASKS
Who held real power in the world in 1900?
Which groups of people challenged the men with power?

EUROPE IN 1900
In 1900 much of Europe was divided between powerful empires which were strictly ruled by monarchs who used their powers to restrict the freedom of their subjects. Some people in states like Russia, Germany and Austria-Hungary wanted to replace their monarchs with a more **democratic** elected government which would do the will of the people. They had little chance of success whilst the rulers controlled the army and the police.

Industry had developed in many parts of Europe and this created a great deal of wealth for the people who owned the factories, but for the new factory workers in the growing towns there was often only low wages and misery. Many workers wanted to challenge the inequalities which industry had created. They formed political parties like the socialists, or **revolutionary** groups known as communists, which aimed to share out the wealth more evenly.

THE WORLD IN 1900
In the previous century European governments had used their new industrial wealth and the weapons which their factories created to conquer much of Africa and Asia. They made these areas into their **colonies** and they hoped to exploit them for cheap labour and for raw materials for their factories. Many of the people in these colonies were anti-colonialist; they hated being dominated by foreigners and they demanded their own governments free from the European powers.

SOURCE A

▲ *Angry French workers fight with soldiers.*

BRITAIN IN 1900

Britain was the first country to develop modern industries. By 1900 it was a very rich and powerful state with many overseas colonies. It was also one of the world's most democratic countries. Unlike many other European states, Britain was ruled by an elected parliament and almost all men over the age of 21 had the vote.

Like most women around the world, British women did not have equal rights to men. They were not allowed to vote and their opportunities in education and employment were severely limited. Most men thought that women should not work because they had less intelligence than men and were better suited to looking after the home and bringing up children. Poorer women who had to work were paid less than men and did jobs which no men wanted.

By the early 1900s this inequality was being challenged by a group of educated women. They formed **suffragist** groups aimed at forcing the government to allow women the right to vote. They believed that women could use their vote to elect a government which would grant them greater equality.

The British Empire was by far the largest of the European empires. In 1900, one in four people and nearly a quarter of the world's land was ruled by Britain.

SOURCE B

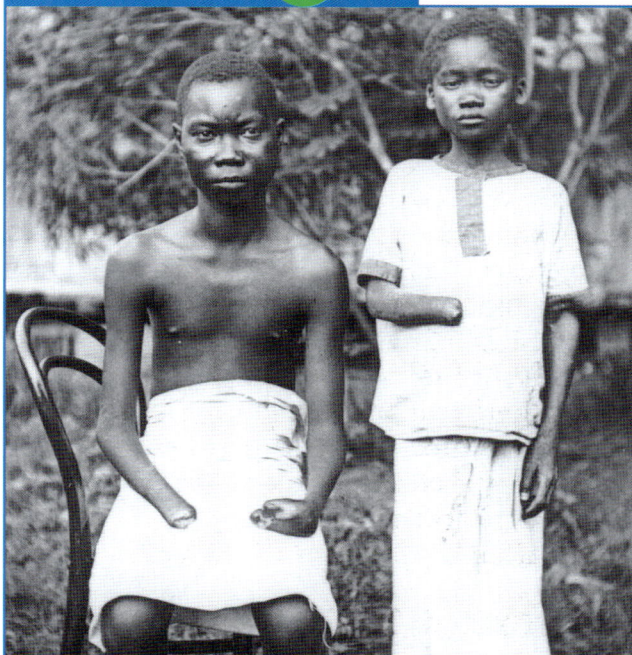

▲ The King of Belgium's rule in the Congo was very brutal. These African workers were punished by having their hands cut off.

SOURCE C

▲ A British painting entitled 'Scene in the Bayswater Omnibus'. How does the artist show inequalities in wealth and the different roles of men and women?

Q

1. Consider the following groups:
■ Democrats
■ Communists and socialists
■ Anti-colonialists
■ British suffragists.

For each group explain who they were, what they wanted and who were their enemies.

2. Use what you know about Britain and the world today to explain which groups have been successful.

Was Mrs Pankhurst right?

SUFFRAGISTS AND SUFFRAGETTES

By 1903 the suffragists had been peacefully campaigning for women's voting rights for nearly fifty years. Although the matter had been brought to parliament several times, it was always voted down and never became law. This made many women very frustrated and convinced some of them that peaceful persuasion would never get them the vote. Led by Emmeline Pankhurst, these women formed the suffragette movement which aimed to get the vote by any means possible, even if it meant breaking the law. Were they right to do this? Did Mrs Pankhurst's methods get the vote for women?

THE SUFFRAGETTES IN ACTION

The leading suffragettes began their new approach by attending political meetings and heckling the speakers. When policemen arrived to throw them out, they would struggle and spit so much that the meeting would be disrupted. Although these tactics were heavily condemned in the newspapers, Pankhurst was delighted. She believed that it was better to get bad publicity than to be ignored.

The suffragettes went on to ever more violent tactics. They slashed paintings in art galleries, smashed shop windows, set fire to a church and chained themselves to the railings of public buildings. When they were arrested they often went on hunger strike and they portrayed government attempts to force-feed them as torture.

During the 1913 Derby a suffragette named Emily Wilding Davison ran in front of the King's horse which fell heavily on her. Many men were outraged because it was a valuable horse. They needn't have worried, the horse was alright, but Emily died a few days later.

SOURCE A

▲ Mrs Pankhurst under arrest.

Emmeline Pankhurst 1858–1928

Born in Manchester and married to a wealthy lawyer. Formed the Women's Social and Political Union (suffragettes for short) in 1903 and adopted illegal protest methods. She was frequently imprisoned and often went on hunger strike. In 1914 she ended all protests and declared that the suffragettes must help the Government to win the war.

◀ A poster from 1912 appealing for votes for women.

SOURCE B

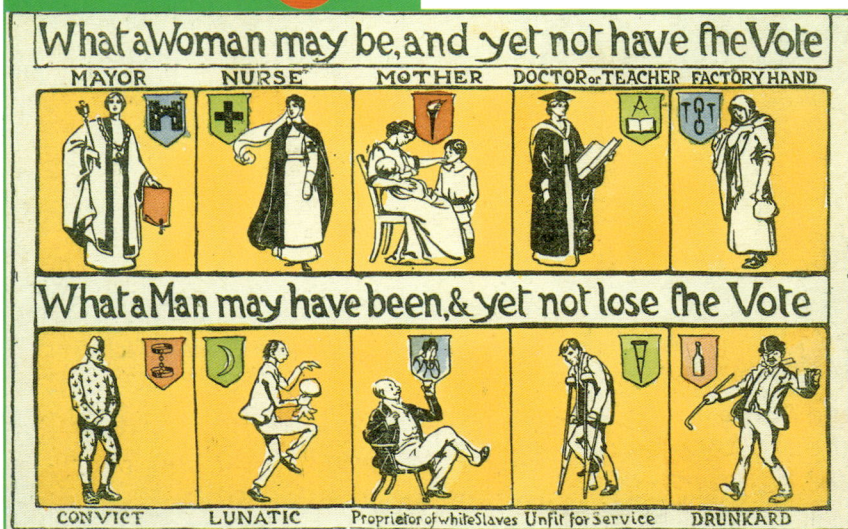

What a Woman may be, and yet not have the Vote

MAYOR   NURSE   MOTHER   DOCTOR or TEACHER   FACTORY HAND

What a Man may have been, & yet not lose the Vote

CONVICT   LUNATIC   Proprietor of white Slaves   Unfit for service   DRUNKARD

SOURCE C

Ladies, if we had the power to grant it, you should have the vote right away. Please do not smash these windows; they are not insured.

▲ *A notice which appeared in a London jeweller's shop in 1912.*

SOURCE E

… it was hardly a tactful way to covert us by burning down our churches and putting bombs in our cathedrals.

▲ *The Bishop of London writing in 1918.*

SOURCE F

The argument of the broken window pane is the most valuable in modern politics.

▲ *Mrs Pankhurst's opinion.*

The first country to give women the vote was New Zealand in 1893. The last European country was Switzerland in 1971.

SOURCE D

▲ *A postcard encouraging people to laugh at the suffragettes. Suffragettes were a popular target for stand-up comedians.*

WOMEN AND THE WAR

In 1914 Britain went to war with Germany. The suffragettes ended their campaign and declared their support for the government in the war effort. Women were to play a vital role, for with so many men called up for the army, it was only through employing over one million women that the country was able to keep going. Their efforts during the war helped to persuade many men that women actually deserved the vote and would use it responsibly. As a result many women over the age of 30 were able to vote for first time in 1918 and ten years later this was extended to all women over the age of 21.

Q 1. Look carefully at **Sources A** and **B**. Which one is the best publicity? Consider the following in your answer:

■ Which is most likely to attract attention?

■ Which is most likely to persuade you that women should have the vote?

Do your answers show that Mrs Pankhurst's activities were effective?

2. Look carefully at how men reacted to the suffragettes in **Sources C, D** and **E**. Do they support Mrs Pankhurst's statement in **Source F**?

Discussion Point

Was Mrs Pankhurst right to use violence? Explain your own *personal opinion*.

Justice for General Dyer?

YOUR MISSION: to find out why a British General ordered his soldiers to shoot hundreds of unarmed Indians; and to discover how people felt about the massacre at the time.

INVESTIGATION

THE AMRITSAR MASSACRE

On 13 April 1919 a crowd of Indians gathered in a walled area of the Indian city of Amritsar. Although the crowd was large, it was very peaceful. It was a market day and many people from the outlying villages were spending the day in the big city. A party of soldiers arrived in the square. Without warning the soldiers fired on the crowd killing nearly five hundred and wounding perhaps another thousand. Why did they do it? The answer lies with their British commander, General Reginald Dyer.

General Reginald Dyer 1864–1927

SOURCE A

▲ *The Amritsar Massacre from the film* Gandhi *made in 1982.*

SOURCE B

I knew that there was going to be trouble in Amritsar and I realised that if I did nothing it would be worse. A military crisis had come ... Amritsar was the storm centre of rebellion and the gathering was a declaration of war by people who hoped I wouldn't dare stop them.

▲ *General Dyer explains why he ordered the massacre.*

COUNTDOWN TO MASSACRE

1914-8
Thousands of Indians fought for Britain in World War One. The British Government encouraged them by announcing changes which would eventually allow India some say in the way it was governed.

1919
British officials feared that India might explode into violence. Harsh new laws were introduced but these only made Indians even more angry.

10 April 1919
In Amritsar an angry crowd of demonstrators was fired on by police. The crowd went on to beat four British men to death. A British woman was severely beaten and left for dead. The Town Hall, post offices and churches were destroyed by the crowd. General Dyer arrived in Amritsar. He was convinced that India was near to revolution.

12 April 1919
General Dyer toured Amritsar warning all Indians against holding protest meetings. He did not visit the area where the massacre was to take place.

SOURCE C

We were not plotting to overthrow the government. The riots were caused by the harsh actions of the British.

▲ *Indian leaders explain the background to the massacre.*

SOURCE F

My father, a mild-tempered man, was almost speechless with indignation on reading in a newspaper of the presentation of a gold sword to General Dyer by a group calling itself the 'Ladies of England'.

▲ *Many British people thought Dyer was a hero. They sent him money and gifts. Here an Indian describes how his father reacted to this news.*

SOURCE G

The British Government today represents satanism. When a government takes up arms against its unarmed subjects then it no longer has a right to govern.

▲ *How the Indian leader Mahatma Gandhi responded to the massacre.*

SOURCE D

The whole rebellion collapsed. The mob that was fired upon dispersed and all trouble ceased in the city of Amritsar, as well as throughout the entire district.

▲ *A British government official describes the effect of the massacre.*

British soldiers force an Indian man to crawl along the street where the British woman was attacked. After the massacre General Dyer ordered that all Indians must bow to every British person they passed. Those who refused were publicly whipped. ➤

SOURCE E

INVESTIGATION

After the massacre General Dyer was forced to retire from the army. Many Indians thought that this was a very light punishment, but some British people believed that Dyer was a hero who should not be punished at all.

1. You are leader of the 'Ladies of England' mentioned in **Source F**. Write the speech which you will give before presenting General Dyer with his sword. Find the evidence to support the following points in your speech:

■ Before the massacre the Indians were the cause of serious trouble.
■ General Dyer's actions both during and after the massacre were justified and reasonable.
■ He has saved India from more trouble in future.

2. You are the Indian man in **Source F**. You believe the complete opposite to the three points made above. Write an angry letter to the leader of the 'Ladies of England' pointing out why they are wrong on all three points.

2 THE ORIGINS OF WORLD WAR ONE

THIS CHAPTER ASKS

How and why did World War One start?
Why did it last so long?
How did ordinary people feel about the start of the war?

AN EXPLOSIVE SITUATION

In 1914 the major powers of Europe were divided into two armed groups known as the Triple Entente (France, Russia and Britain) and the Triple **Alliance** (Germany, Austria-Hungary and Italy). The fear and distrust between these alliances made war a real possibility. It seemed that European leaders were sitting on dangerous powder kegs which could destroy them all. All that was needed was a spark.

Read THE SPARK and see how Austria reacted, then follow the trail around Europe to see how World War One began.

NEW WORDS

ALLIANCE: an agreement between countries to help each other in a war.
MOBILISATION: assembling an army to attack another country.

Q

1. Why did the following countries quarrel before 1914?
■ Serbia and Austria-Hungary
■ Austria-Hungary and Russia
■ France and Germany
■ Britain and Germany.

2. Did being in an alliance mean that you had to get involved in a war? Use the illustration to explain your answer.

3. Why do you think Britain got involved?

We feel threatened because Germany has started to build a powerful navy. We would like to stay out of this, but we have promised to help Belgium.

4 August 1914. Britain declared war on Germany.

Britain

We hate Germany. They beat us in the last war and took our land. We want it back.

France

Why did Schlieffen's plan fail?

THE SCHLIEFFEN PLAN

Germany's plans for war were probably the most detailed and thorough ever devised. They were the creation of top commander Alfred von Schlieffen, but he died before they were carried out. In the first weeks of the war, the fate of Europe rested in the hands of a dead man. Had Schlieffen got all his calculations right?

HOW THE SCHLIEFFEN PLAN WOULD WORK

1. Germany must avoid a war on two fronts by beating France before Russia can intervene. Most of the German Army would march through Belgium and capture Paris.
2. Weak German forces would hold the French up on the frontier and a small German army would try to hold up any Russian advance in the East.

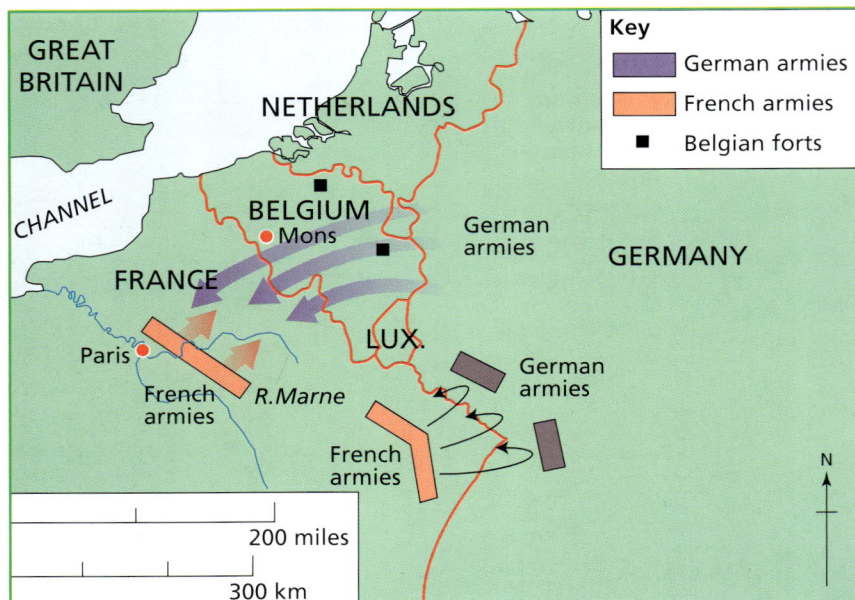

▲ *Alfred von Schlieffen. 1833–1913.*

◄ *German army movements August to September 1914.*

SOURCE A

Schlieffen's whole plan assumed the absence of any enemy – an astonishing assumption for a commander to make …

▲ *A.J.P. Taylor. From* The First World War.

SOURCE B

The Schlieffen Plan simply stretched the German army too far. By the time the troops reached the River Marne, they were totally exhausted. It is doubtful whether they would have been able to take Paris even if it had been open for them to do so.

▲ *From* The Great War and the Shaping of the 20th Century. *Jay Winter and Blaine Baggett.*

SCHLIEFFEN'S MISTAKES

Almost as soon as the plan was launched, Schlieffen's careful calculations fell apart. Russia **mobilised** far faster than he thought possible and so many German troops had to be sent away from the war against France to fight an invading Russian army in the East. The Belgians put up unexpectedly strong resistance and held up the German advance for three vital days. He thought that Britain would not intervene to help Belgium, and even if it did, the British army would be too small to have any effect. Instead, the unprovoked invasion brought Britain into the war and although the British Expeditionary Force was small, it was also highly trained and was able to hold up the German advance at Mons before retreating in good order.

THE BIGGEST MISTAKE

Schlieffen imagined that the German advance would be so rapid that the French would be unable to respond. In reality the French were able to use trains to rush men back from the frontier and taxis to bring troops from Paris. They caught the Germans at the River Marne and, after a three-day battle, halted their advance. Schlieffen's plan for a quick victory had failed. The war would have to be decided by living men.

> The Germans had long viewed the small British army as a joke. They said that if the British army landed on the coast of Germany, they would send a policeman to arrest it.

THE LAST MISTAKE

Like many other commanders at the time, Schlieffen imagined that the war could be won by the aggressive charges of bayonet-armed infantry and thousands of cavalrymen armed with swords and lances. When these tactics were tried, however, the attackers were usually shot to pieces because new weapons such as the quick-firing rifle, machine-guns and the heavy artillery piece made an advance across open ground all but impossible.

In this **stalemate** neither side could advance so they both set out to hold what ground they had by digging trenches. By the end of 1914 both sides in the West had a line of trenches which stretched from Switzerland to the Channel Coast. Between the enemy armies was an area of no-man's land that was almost impossible to cross.

SOURCE C

▲ *Canadian troops are attacked by Germans in early 1915. Although they were out-numbered, the Canadians' machine-guns and quick-firing rifles helped them defeat the German attack.*

Q

1. Explain why Russia, Belgium and Britain were each able to ruin Schlieffen's plans.

2. How do **Sources A** and **B** disagree about the reasons why the Schlieffen Plan failed?

3. The Schlieffen Plan failed for the following reasons:

- Enemy resistance
- Mistakes by German commanders
- Distance
- New weapons.

Explain each factor and say whether you think Schlieffen can be blamed. Finish by suggesting any change which you might make to the Plan to make it more successful.

11

Franz Ferdinand's final day

YOUR MISSION: to investigate the murder of Archduke Franz Ferdinand. The results of your investigation could pull Europe from the brink of war and change the course of history.

On 28 June 1914 the heir to the Austro-Hungarian throne, Archduke Franz Ferdinand, and his wife Sophie were shot dead in the Bosnian town of Sarajevo. The killer was Gavrilo Princip, a young man who believed that Bosnia should leave the Austro-Hungarian Empire and become part of neighbouring Serbia.

SOURCE A

▲ *The Archduke's car passes through a street in Sarajevo.*

SOURCE B

```
Name:   Gavrilo Princip
Born:   Bosnia
Age:    19

Member of a pro-Serbian
political group which has
links with Serbian
terrorists. Visited Serbia
regularly between 1912
and 1914.
```

▲ *What we know of the murderer.*

SOURCE C

I drew the revolver and raised it against the automobile without aiming. I even turned my head as I shot. I let go two shots one after the other, but I am not certain whether I shot twice or more often, because I was very excited.

▲ *Princip's account of the murder.*

SOURCE D

1910 *Visit of the Emperor Franz Josef*
Entire route of visit lined with double cordon of soldiers. Hundreds of suspected terrorists arrested.

1914 *Visit of Franz Ferdinand*
70,000 soldiers camped outside the city.
120 policemen to guard the four-mile route.

▲ *Arrangements for two Imperial visits to Sarajevo.*

SOURCE E

Precautions? Security measures? ... I do not care the tiniest bit about this. Everywhere one is in God's hands. Look, out of this bush here at the right some chap could jump at me ... Fears and precautions paralyse one's life.

▲ *Archduke Franz Ferdinand's attitude to security. April 1914.*

INVESTIGATION

SOURCE F

This is not the crime of a single fanatic; assassination represents Serbia's declaration of war on Austria-Hungary … If we don't do something about this we will have trouble from the Czechs, Russians, Romanians and Italians … Austria-Hungary must wage war for political reasons.

▲ *Conrad von Hotzendorf. Austrian Army Commander-in-Chief. July 1914.*

SOURCE G

Security on the 28th June will be in the hands of fate.

▲ *A Senior Policeman in Sarajevo. Speaking in early June 1914.*

SOURCE H

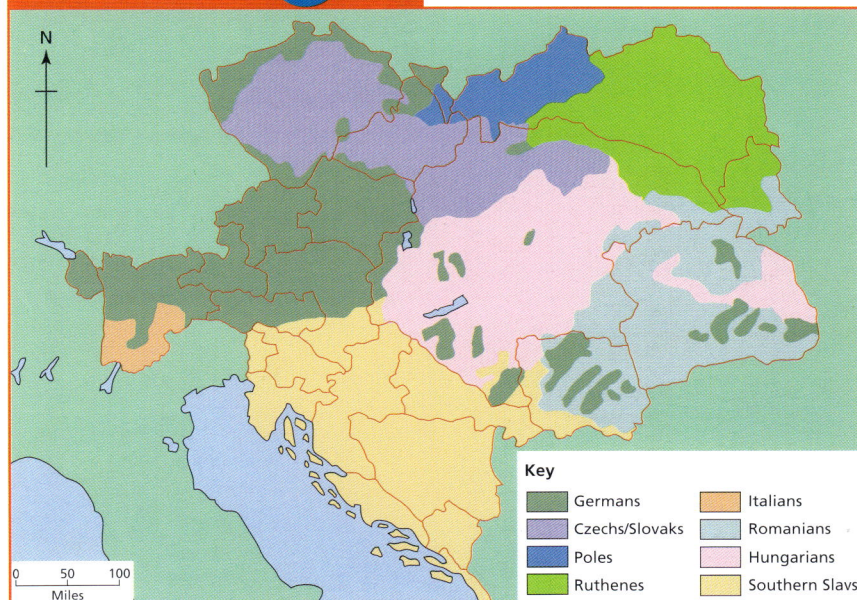

Key
- Germans
- Czechs/Slovaks
- Poles
- Ruthenes
- Italians
- Romanians
- Hungarians
- Southern Slavs

▲ *Austria-Hungary was a state made up of many different nationalities.*

SOURCE I

… many details prove that the Serbian government were not involved and actually did not want the Archduke to be assassinated. The Serbs were exhausted by two previous wars. The most hot-headed among them might have paused at the thought of war with Austria-Hungary who were so overwhelmingly superior.

▲ *The opinion of the German minister in Serbia. Germany was a close friend of Austria-Hungary.*

INVESTIGATION

You are the investigator!

To write your report you will need to consider the following questions. Each answer will form a paragraph in your finished report.

1. Examine **Sources A** to **G**, then answer the following questions:

a. Do you feel that Princip was a professional terrorist who may have been trained in Serbia?

b. Were the security arrangements adequate?

c. If the security arrangements were poor, who is to blame? Consider **Sources E** and **G**.

2. Look carefully at **Sources F, H** and **I**.

a. Was Serbia to blame for the assassination? Explain your answer.

b. Should Austria-Hungary be prepared to go to war?

c. Why might Austria-Hungary go to war even if Serbia were not involved in the assassination?

Why did men volunteer?

YOUR MISSION: to write a speech persuading young men to volunteer to join the army.

You are Mayor of the small northern town of Grimdale and you are determined that more young men should volunteer to join the army from your town than from any other in the locality. At great expense you decide to hire the popular public speaker Horatio Bottomley to come to the Town Hall to boost recruitment. You even have the hall decorated with recruitment posters. Then, with one hour to the meeting your receive news that Bottomley can't make it. You will have to make the speech yourself. You anxiously look around the hall for inspiration …

Daddy, what did YOU do in the Great War?

REMEMBER BELGIUM

ENLIST TO-DAY

YOUR COUNTRY'S CALL

Isn't this worth fighting for?

ENLIST NOW

INVESTIGATION

You are to make a speech!

1. Start by introducing yourself.

■ Who are you?

■ Why are you here?

2. Then use each of the posters which you can see on the wall as the basis for each paragraph of your speech. Try to put the poster's message into words.

■ Consider, who is the poster aimed at?

■ What does it ask them to do?

■ Why does it say that men should join the army?

■ What is to be defended?

■ Who will be impressed?

■ What are the enemy like?

■ What is the war like?

3. Finish your speech by asking why men should join up. Use each poster to provide the final answer.

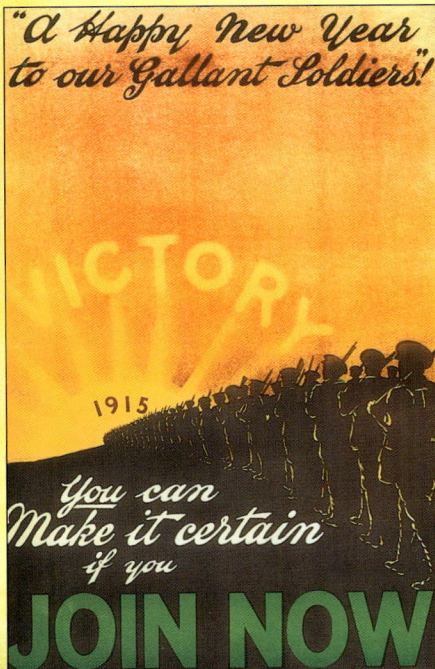

"A Happy New Year to our Gallant Soldiers!"

VICTORY

1915

You can make it certain if you

JOIN NOW

GO!

IT'S YOUR DUTY LAD

JOIN TO-DAY

3 LIVING AND DYING IN THE TRENCHES

THIS CHAPTER ASKS
What was it like to live in the trenches?
How did the commanders try to break the stalemate?
Why did they fail?

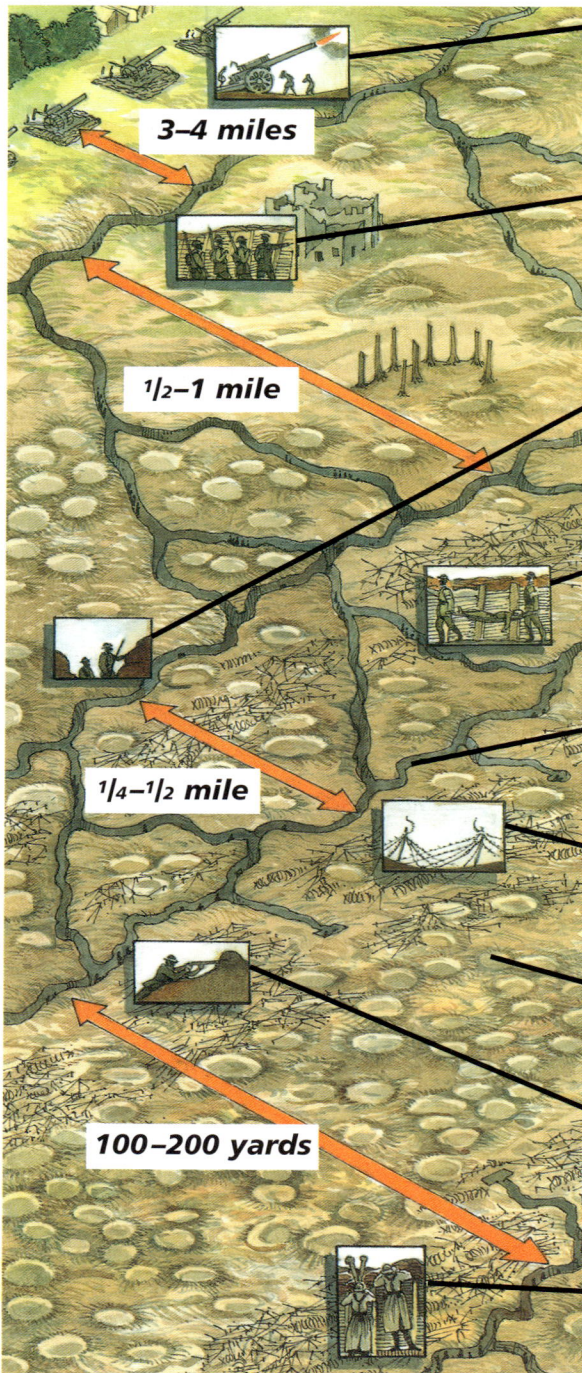

3–4 miles

¹/₂–1 mile

¹/₄–¹/₂ mile

100–200 yards

▲ A view of the trenches.

Behind the lines. *Army camps, huge stock piles of stores and thousands of enormous guns, some of which which could fire on the German line from as far away as six miles.*

Reserve trenches. *A soldier might spend eight days per month here. These trenches were used to build up forces for an attack or launch a counter-attack if the front-line trenches were threatened.*

Support trench. *A soldier might spend four days per month here. More comfortable and slightly less dangerous than the front-line trench.*

Communication trenches. *Used to bring up supplies usually at night. During a battle ammunition and reinforcements had priority over the evacuation of the wounded.*

Front-line trench. *Most uncomfortable and dangerous. A soldier might spend four days here per month.*

Barbed wire. *With gaps to allow patrols in and out. Tin cans were sometimes hung on the wire to give early warning of an attack.*

No Man's Land. *Usually deserted during the day, at night it was patrolled by small parties of well-armed men.*

Advanced listening post. *Usually a shell crater occupied by two or three men during the hours of darkness. Many were so close that they could hear German soldiers snoring.*

German front-line trench. *Almost always better constructed than the British trenches with deep dug-outs to protect the soldiers from shelling.*

NEW WORDS

SHRAPNEL: Pieces of exploding artillery shells.
DUG-OUTS: Underground caverns where soldiers would shelter from bombardment.
TANK-TRAPS: Specially dug ditches which tanks were unable to cross without getting stuck.

LIFE IN THE TRENCHES

For most soldiers, life in the trenches followed a set routine. They would be awake half an hour before dawn and would stand by in preparation for a possible enemy attack. The remainder of the day was divided equally between sentry-duty, work (filling sandbags and mending trenches) and rest. Throughout the day there might be a series of inspections from officers and sergeants.

The greatest problem faced by the ordinary soldier was the sheer discomfort of living in the trenches. Men used to city life could find the intense cold unbearable and this was made even worse by rain and mud which left them wet for days on end. Whilst officers had their own private **dug-outs**, the men had to make do with a ledge dug into the side of the trench, so prolonged sleep was almost impossible. Added to the misery of exhaustion, was the problem of lice which infested everyone and giant rats which multiplied and grew to enormous sizes by eating the corpses in No Man's Land. Some of these rats were so large and fierce that they were even known to attack wounded and sleeping men.

SOURCE A

▲ *British soldiers in a flooded reserve area.*

SOURCE B

The cold crept under our clothes, our fingers and joints ached with it; it seemed to congeal our blood and kill the very marrow of our bones.

▲ *A soldier describes the cold in the trenches during the winter of 1917.*

Q **Discussion Point**

In 1914 thousands of men volunteered to fight. Do you think the same would happen today if there were a war?

SOURCE C

◀ *A German corpse decaying in the trenches. The rats have already eaten away the face.*

THE BIG PICTURE

SOURCE D

▲ *A wounded soldier being evacuated from the front-line.*

SOURCE E

December 9th 1915. Hazy. Cool. One leaning against a tree. One fifty yards right. Fell across a log. Shot three successive helpers.
December 16th 1916. Clear. Fine. Good hunting. Sixteen good shots. Seven known hits and feel sure of four more.

▲ *Excerpts from a British sniper's diary.*

The biggest guns used in World War One were three guns which the Germans used to bombard Paris in 1918. They could hurl a shell the weight of a small car 71 miles. The French thought there was only one gun. They nicknamed it Big Bertha.

DEATH IN THE TRENCHES

Even in the quietest sector of the front the soldier in the trenches was in constant danger from the enemy. Both sides used specially trained snipers who could hit a man's head from up to half a mile away and there was always the threat of a sudden short bombardment from the enemy's big guns. The **shrapnel** from the guns' exploding shells could cut men in two or the explosion could bury them alive. Such was the power of the big guns that even those who had a near miss might be killed by the shock of the explosion which could burst their internal organs without leaving a mark on them.

SOURCE F

Pratt was hopeless. His head was shattered. Splatterings of brain lay in a pool under him... it took over two hours before he died in a crowded place where perhaps a dozen men sat with the smell of blood... gurgling and moaning from his lips, now high and liquid, now low and dry – a death rattle fit for the most blood-thirsty novelist.

▲ *Death of a British soldier hit by a German sniper.*

NIGHT IN THE TRENCHES

The hours of darkness were the most active and tense time in the trenches. Nervous sentries scanned the dark horizon for any sign of enemy activity. Small groups of heavily armed men would often clash as they patrolled No Man's Land. Both sides sent raiding parties to the enemy trenches in order to capture prisoners for interrogation. These trench-raids often involved vicious hand-to-hand combat with knives, clubs and spades.

THE EXPERIENCE OF BATTLE

Throughout the war, generals attempted to break through the enemy's trenches by launching massive frontal assaults. Sometimes these attacks might take the front-line trench, but they rarely got any further and were usually driven out by a counter-attack. For many of the men the experience of battle was one of senseless sacrifice. They were ordered out of their trenches to cross No Man's Land in a hail of machine-gun bullets and shrapnel. The result was usually slaughter, with thousands killed outright and many more left to die of wounds in No Man's Land. Until the last few months of the war no breakthrough was ever achieved.

SOURCE H

▲ A club used by British soldiers in trench raids.

CHANGING ATTITUDES TO THE WAR

As the war dragged on with no end in sight, many soldiers came to resent the politicians who had sent them to war and the generals whose plans led to such heavy casualties with no hope of victory. Only loyalty to their mates and fierce army discipline, which included the firing squad for desertion, kept them at their posts. They simply wanted to survive the war and return home.

THE COST OF TRENCH LIFE

Many soldiers lost their lives on quiet days when no particular battle was taking place and others suffered from a wide variety of physical illnesses brought on by conditions in the trenches. But there were also less obvious casualties brought about by exposure to constant danger and sudden death; thousands of men suffered a form of nervous breakdown known as shellshock, and even those who seemed to escape the war unscathed could suffer in later life. Ten years after the war 65,000 British ex-soldiers were in mental homes.

SOURCE G

Old soldiers say bayonneting was like sticking a knife into butter. The only problem was getting the blade back out because the skin and muscle closed on the bayonet. Thus the half twist which men in training were taught.

▲ How to use a bayonet. From **Death's Men,** by Dennis Winter. 1978.

SOURCE I

We're here, because we're here,
Because we're here,
Because we're here,
(repeat many times)

▲ A British soldiers' song. What does it suggest about their attitude to the war?

Q You are an old soldier who has to introduce fresh young soldiers to the trenches. Write a three-page illustrated leaflet explaining the following:

■ How to find your way around the trench system

■ Dangers and how to avoid them

■ Discomforts and how to make life tolerable.

Use both the text and the sources to provide as detailed a guide as possible.

The ultimate weapon?

After 1914 both sides looked to technology and science for a new weapon which could break the stalemate.

GAS

On the 22 April 1915 German soldiers opened hundreds of canisters and allowed the first poison gas to blow over the Allied trenches at Ypres. The effect was devastating. A whole section of Allied line was left defenceless as men choked or ran in terror from the gas. The Germans were not prepared for the enormous success of their new weapon, however, and the chance to break through was lost because there were not enough troops ready for an attack.

Despite this wasted opportunity, German inventors continued to develop poison gas, and they soon discovered a way to deliver a range of ever more horrific gases from artillery shells. Phosgene gas attacked the lungs, making them fill up and drown the victim in his own body fluids, whilst contact with mustard gas could burn skin away to the bone.

British soldiers were able to protect their lungs in early gas attacks by urinating in a handkerchief and holding it over their mouths. At Nieuport in France, Scottish soldiers who wore kilts, protected their bare legs from mustard gas by wearing lady's drawers.

SOURCE A

Gas horns would be honked, empty brass shell-cases beaten, rifles emptied and the mad cry would be taken up. For miles around scared soldiers woke up in the midst of frightful pandemonium and put on their masks, only to hear a few minutes later the cry of 'All safe'. Gas shock was as frequent as shellshock.

▲ *A gas alarm in the trenches.*

SOURCE B

▲ **British soldiers blinded by gas are led away from the front lines.**

Despite its early impact, poison gas was never to become a war-winning weapon. Even the slightest breeze could make its effects unpredictable and it often became as big a problem for the defenders as it was for the attackers. The Allies were quick to act against the threat and, within a week of the first attack, the British had distributed over 300,000 gas masks amongst their troops. They also developed their own poison gas production. In the end, gas did nothing to shorten the war, it only made the conflict more horrific for the ordinary soldier.

SOURCE C

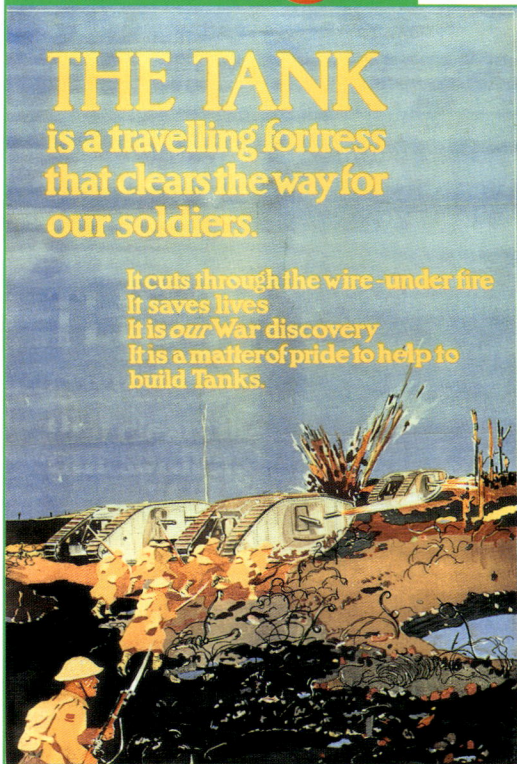

THE TANK is a travelling fortress that clears the way for our soldiers.

It cuts through the wire–under fire
It saves lives
It is *our* War discovery
It is a matter of pride to help to build Tanks.

▲ *A British poster appealing for money to build tanks.*

SOURCE D

The tanks' military impact in France was minor but on the home front it boosted morale enormously.

▲ Timewatch, *BBC Television, 1998.*

TANKS

On 15 September 1916, German troops on the Somme were terrified by the sight of huge mechanical monsters lumbering across the battlefield spitting shells and machine-gun bullets. These were the first tanks which were developed in great secrecy in Britain during the previous year. They tore into the German lines, smashing machine-gun nests and emptying trenches, yet despite the fear which they created the tanks had little effect on the outcome of the battle. They had been sent in as a last resort by a commander desperate for a breakthrough and there was never enough of them to make any real difference. The only effect of their appearance was to give the Germans warning of what they might expect in future.

The British soon discovered that their tanks had a number of important weaknesses. They were mechanically unreliable and, because of their weight, they often got stuck in the mud of No Man's Land. With a top cross-country speed of four miles per hour, they were easy targets for artillery and their thin armour was not even guaranteed to keep the crews completely safe against rifle fire. The Germans responded to the tank threat with specially dug **tank-traps**, heavy anti-tank rifles and armour piercing ammunition. Only when the Allied commanders had a large number of tanks and knew how to use them properly could they be expected to change the course of the war.

Q **1.** Does the fact that gas and tanks did not win the war mean they were not significant weapons? Answer this question by referring to **Sources A to D**.

2. Complete the table below, then use it to explain why tanks and gas failed to end the war.

	Gas	Tank
How did commanders misuse the weapon?		
What were its weaknesses?		
How did the enemy counter the weapon?		

Breakthrough on the Somme?

YOUR MISSION: to report on the battle plan for the Somme Offensive.

In 1916 the British Army planned to win the war in one major battle. You are a high-ranking Army Intelligence Officer. It is your job to work through all the available information on the progress of the battle and provide the Commander-in-Chief, General Haig, with reports and recommendations. Look carefully at the battle plan below, then review all the information in the sources before writing your report.

Plan for the Somme Offensive

TOP SECRET

1. A huge new army of volunteers will be recruited.

2. Supplies and men will assemble to attack the Somme sector of the front.

3. German defences will be bombarded with over one and a half million shells for seven days before the attack.

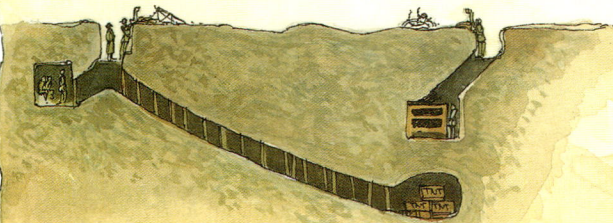

4. The bombardment will destroy the German defences, break their barbed wire and kill most of their defenders.

5. Three big mines and seven small ones will be dug under German strong points to be exploded just before the attack.

6. The new army will advance across No Man's Land and occupy the German defences.

Signed *Douglas Haig*
COMMANDER-IN-CHIEF
British Army

SOURCE A

The German machine-guns and infantry must have been preserved owing to their deep dug-outs. These were numerous and elaborate, most of them thirty or forty feet below ground level, with two or three entrances. The enemy wire entanglements had everywhere been completely destroyed by our artillery.

▲ *Lieutenant B.L. Gordon, King's Own Yorkshire Light Infantry.*

SOURCE C

We went down into a (German) dug-out and actually found the electric lights still burning. So much for the artillery preparation.

▲ *Private A. McMullen, Donegal and Fermanagh Volunteers.*

SOURCE D

When the English started advancing we were very worried; they looked as though they must overrun our trenches. We were very surprised to see them walking, we had never seen that before. The officers were in front. I noticed one of them walking calmly carrying a walking stick. When we started firing, we just had to load and reload. They went down in their hundreds. You didn't have to aim, we just fired into them. If only they had run, they would have overwhelmed us.

▲ *Private Karl Blenk, 169th Regiment. German Army.*

SOURCE E

I could see away to my left and right, long lines of men. Then I heard the 'patter patter' of machine-guns in the distance. By the time I'd gone another ten yards there seemed to be only a few men left around me; by the time I'd gone twenty yards I seemed to be on my own. Then I was hit myself.

▲ *Sergeant J. Galloway, 3rd Battalion. Tyneside Irish.*

SOURCE B

I was in the first wave. My first impression was the sight of unexploded mortar bombs... they were supposed to destroy the German wire which was almost untouched. I doubt if one had exploded.

▲ *Private G.S. Young, North Staffordshire Regiment.*

INVESTIGATION

You are the investigator!

You must prepare a report for the British commander Douglas Haig. Write a paragraph on each of the following:

- The main aims for the day and why there should be no German opposition.
- Did the bombardment achieve its planned purpose?
- How did so many Germans survive the bombardment?
- Why were the surviving Germans able to inflict so many casualties?

Finish your report with a final paragraph which puts forward your proposals for solving any the problems which you have discovered in the planning of the first day's attack.

THE END OF THE WAR

THIS CHAPTER ASKS
Why did Germany lose the war?
How was Germany affected by the defeat?

NEW WORDS

ARMISTICE: a cease-fire.

BLOCKADE: preventing goods and people from getting in or out of a country.

THE GERMAN CHANCE OF VICTORY

In April 1917 the USA came into the war against Germany. It seemed that with its enormous industry and manpower the Americans would make an Allied victory inevitable, but the USA was unprepared for war and it would take a long time for them to recruit, train and equip an army large enough to confront the Germans in France. There was just enough time to defeat the Allies before the Americans could have a real impact. Germany decided to risk everything on a quick victory.

Russia withdrew from the war at the end of 1917, and this freed up more German troops for the big offensive in France. The bravest men in every German unit were formed into special stormtrooper groups. They were given the best available weapons and training so that they could spearhead the attack.

SOURCE A

TREAT 'EM ROUGH!
JOIN THE TANKS
United States Tank Corps.
MEN NOW ENLISTING AT ARMY RECRUITING STATION

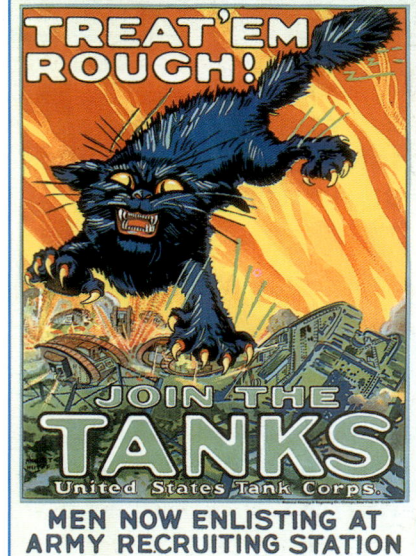

▲ An American recruitment poster for the Tank Corps.

SOURCE B

▲ German stormtroopers go over the top on the first day of the March offensive.

THE MARCH OFFENSIVE

In March 1918 the stormtroopers launched an all-out attack on Allied lines. Once again German soldiers reached the River Marne near Paris, but their attack slowed and finally stopped. The Allied line buckled, but did not break; the attack had cost Germany the lives of thousands of its best soldiers. In August 1918 an Allied counter-attack using tanks, aircraft and fresh American soldiers sent the Germans into full retreat.

SOURCE C

▲ *German soldiers return home in 1918. In many places they were treated like heroes. They blamed civilian politicians for their defeat and refused to admit that they had been beaten.*

THE GERMAN REVOLUTION

Since the start of the war, German ports had been blockaded by the British Royal Navy whose aim was to starve the Germans of food and the raw materials on which their factories depended. The **blockade** took a long time to have any effect, but by 1918 German war production was already slowing and food was becoming scarce, making life miserable for civilians. Meanwhile, Germany's allies were dropping out of the war. In September 1918 Bulgaria surrendered, and at the beginning of November Austria-Hungary simply fell apart as its many different nationalities attempted to form their own independent countries.

The failure of the March Offensive deeply demoralised German civilians and sailors who now both realised that defeat was inevitable. In October 1918 the German fleet was ordered to sail out of port to challenge the British, but most sailors saw no point in sacrificing themselves for a cause which they thought was already lost. The sailors mutinied and started a revolution which soon began to spread to ordinary civilians in the cities.

With the army being pushed back and the civilian population demanding peace at any price, German leaders had no choice but to ask for an **armistice**. The fighting stopped at 11 am on 11 November 1918.

SOURCE D

Nothing important was lost by the failure of the March Offensive. The German line was still unbroken and although they lost the land which they had gained earlier, they simply withdrew to stronger positions. The real effect was psychological. The failure shattered faith in victory which, until that moment, had carried the Germans forward. They realised that the decision had gone against them. They no longer wanted to win. They wanted only to end the war.

▲ *A.J.P. Taylor, from* **The First World War.**

Q 1. Were returning German soldiers right to feel that they were not defeated in 1918?

2. Explain how each of the following contributed to Germany's defeat:

- The Allied blockade of Germany
- US entry into the war
- The failure of the March Offensive
- The mutiny of the German fleet.

Which do you think was most important?

YOUR MISSION: to discover how Germany and its government would be affected by the Treaty of Versailles.

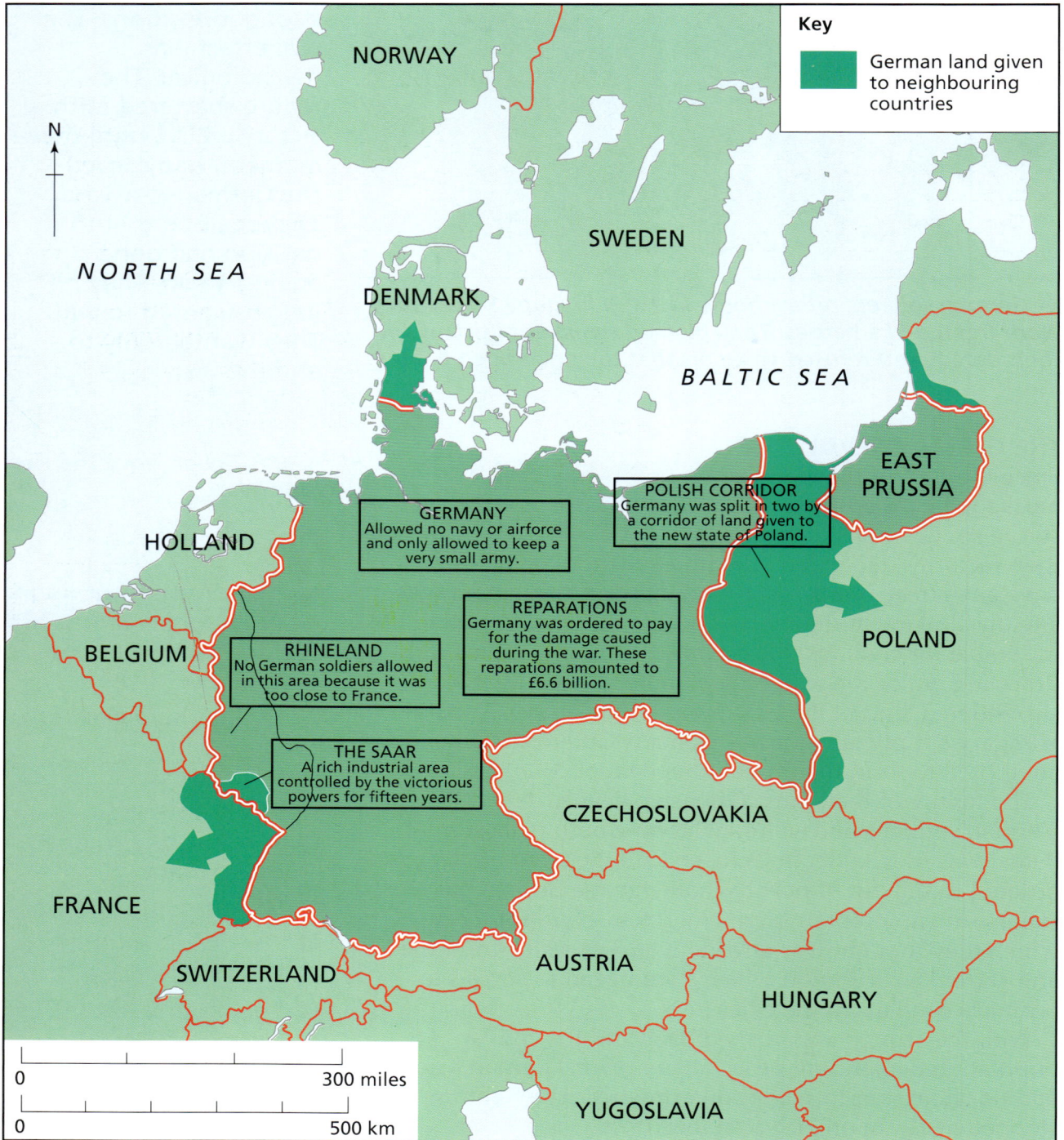

Key

German land given to neighbouring countries

NORWAY

SWEDEN

NORTH SEA

DENMARK

BALTIC SEA

N

EAST PRUSSIA

POLISH CORRIDOR
Germany was split in two by a corridor of land given to the new state of Poland.

HOLLAND

GERMANY
Allowed no navy or airforce and only allowed to keep a very small army.

BELGIUM

REPARATIONS
Germany was ordered to pay for the damage caused during the war. These reparations amounted to £6.6 billion.

POLAND

RHINELAND
No German soldiers allowed in this area because it was too close to France.

THE SAAR
A rich industrial area controlled by the victorious powers for fifteen years.

CZECHOSLOVAKIA

FRANCE

SWITZERLAND

AUSTRIA

HUNGARY

0   300 miles

0   500 km

YUGOSLAVIA

In June 1919 the new democratic German government (known as the Weimar Republic) was forced to sign the **Treaty** of Versailles which imposed very harsh peace terms on Germany. You are an adviser to Karl Ebert, the first President of the Weimar Republic. He has asked you to discover the likely effects of the Treaty on his government. He is particularly interested in the future state of economy and the strength of German military defences. He fears that these two factors might make his government unpopular. Look carefully at the map on page 26.

Look carefully at the map on page 26.

NEW WORDS

REPARATIONS: money which Germany had to pay to repair damage in the countries which won the war.
TREATY: an agreement between countries.

INVESTIGATION

You are the investigator!

Complete the following table. Then use it to write a letter advising Ebert on the future economic, military and political problems his government might face.

The Treaty meant …	Economic effect	Military effect
Loss of land (including the Saar)	Loss of farmland, industry and raw materials like coal mines. Fewer workers to pay taxes. Country will be much poorer.	Smaller population means fewer soldiers available for the army. Loss of industry and raw materials might make it more difficult.
No German soldiers in the Rhineland		
Creation of Polish Corridor		
Reparations		
Military restrictions		
Possible effects on German public opinion of government		

5 THE CHALLENGE OF COMMUNISM

NEW WORDS

BOLSHEVIKS: The Russian Communist Party
PROVISIONAL: Temporary.
REVOLUTION: The violent overthrow of a government.

WHAT IS COMMUNISM?

Communism is a political theory which says that there would be no poverty if all wealth and property were shared by the whole community instead of being owned by private individuals. A German writer named Karl Marx (1818–83) was the most important communist thinker.

RUSSIA UNDER THE TSAR

The world's first successful communist **revolution** occurred in Russia. In Russian cities the workers were very unhappy with their working conditions and their poor wages. They felt badly treated but they could do nothing about it. Russia was ruled by a Tsar (emperor) whose powerful army and police force dealt brutally with all opposition.

THE RUSSIAN REVOLUTION

In 1914 Russia became involved in World War One and quickly suffered a series of disastrous defeats which made the Tsar very unpopular with the ordinary soldiers. Meanwhile, the economy was badly disrupted by the war and this meant that many workers in the cities could not get enough food. In February 1917 the hungry workers of St. Petersburg rioted and instead of putting down the rioters, the army simply joined them. The Tsar had clearly lost control; he was forced to give up the throne and hand over power to a group of middle-class politicians who formed a **Provisional** Government.

What did Marx think would happen?

Capitalism is wrong. Factory workers do all the work but the owners (known as capitalists) keep most of the profits.

One day the workers will unite and overthrow the owners.

Then they will create a new communist government where everyone will work and get an equal share of the benefits.

THE COMMUNISTS TAKE POWER

The new Provisional Government made many mistakes and it was soon very unpopular with the workers and peasants. It decided to continue with the war and this led to even more defeats and food shortages in the cities. Lenin and his **Bolshevik** party opposed the government and demanded immediate peace. By October 1917 the Provisional Government had become so unpopular that Lenin was able to use his armed supporters to seize power and make Russia a communist country.

Many capitalist countries distrusted and disliked this new state. They wondered whether Communism could really work. If it did, they feared that it might eventually threaten them with the world-wide revolution that Marx had predicted.

Q

1. Use the information in this chapter to explain why Marx thought that a workers' revolution would create a better society.

2. Put the following statements in chronological order and then complete them:

- Other countries feared and distrusted Russia because …
- The Tsar lost power because …
- Lenin took power, he wanted a communist country where …
- The Provisional Government lost power because …
- Karl Marx was a communist, this meant that he believed …

3. Use **Sources A** and **B** to complete the following statements:

- A Russian communist, 'I hate and fear the Western capitalist countries because …'
- A Western capitalist, 'I hate and fear communist Russia because …'

SOURCE A

▲ *A communist poster from the early 1920s. It reads 'Red Moscow is the Heart of the World Revolution'.*

SOURCE B

A cartoon showing Russia's attitude towards the capitalist countries. The fat people are rich capitalists, who live well while poor workers starve. ▶

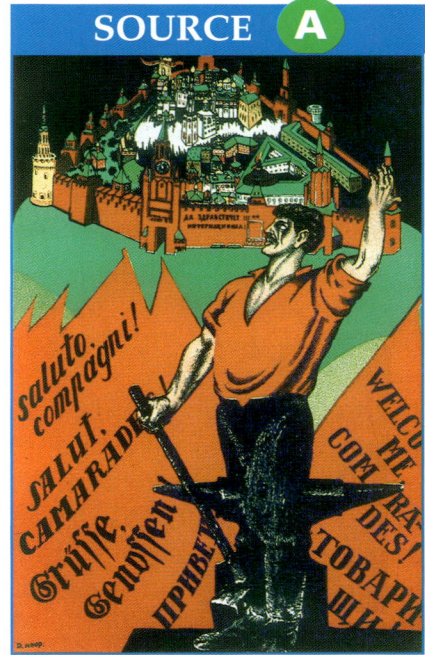

The fall of the Winter Palace

YOUR MISSION: to discover the real story behind what happened at the storming of the Winter Palace in October 1917.

We know that the **Bolsheviks** seized power by taking over the Winter Palace where the Provisional Government was meeting on the night of 26 October 1917. But what actually happened? How did the Bolsheviks take power?

You have been asked by a Hollywood film producer to investigate the possibility of making a big budget movie about the events of October 1917. The producer has just seen Sergei Eisenstein's film, *October* (made in Russia in 1927), and is very excited about this project. He wants to make a film which tells the real story but is exciting enough to attract film-goers. Is this possible?

Sergei Eisenstein was allowed to borrow soldiers from the army to restage the storming of the Winter Palace. They used live ammunition in some of the scenes and there were more people shot during the film than were actually wounded during the real events of October 1917.

Bolshevik soldiers and sailors storm the gate of the Winter Palace. ▼

▲ *Troops loyal to the Provisional Government defend the Winter Palace.*

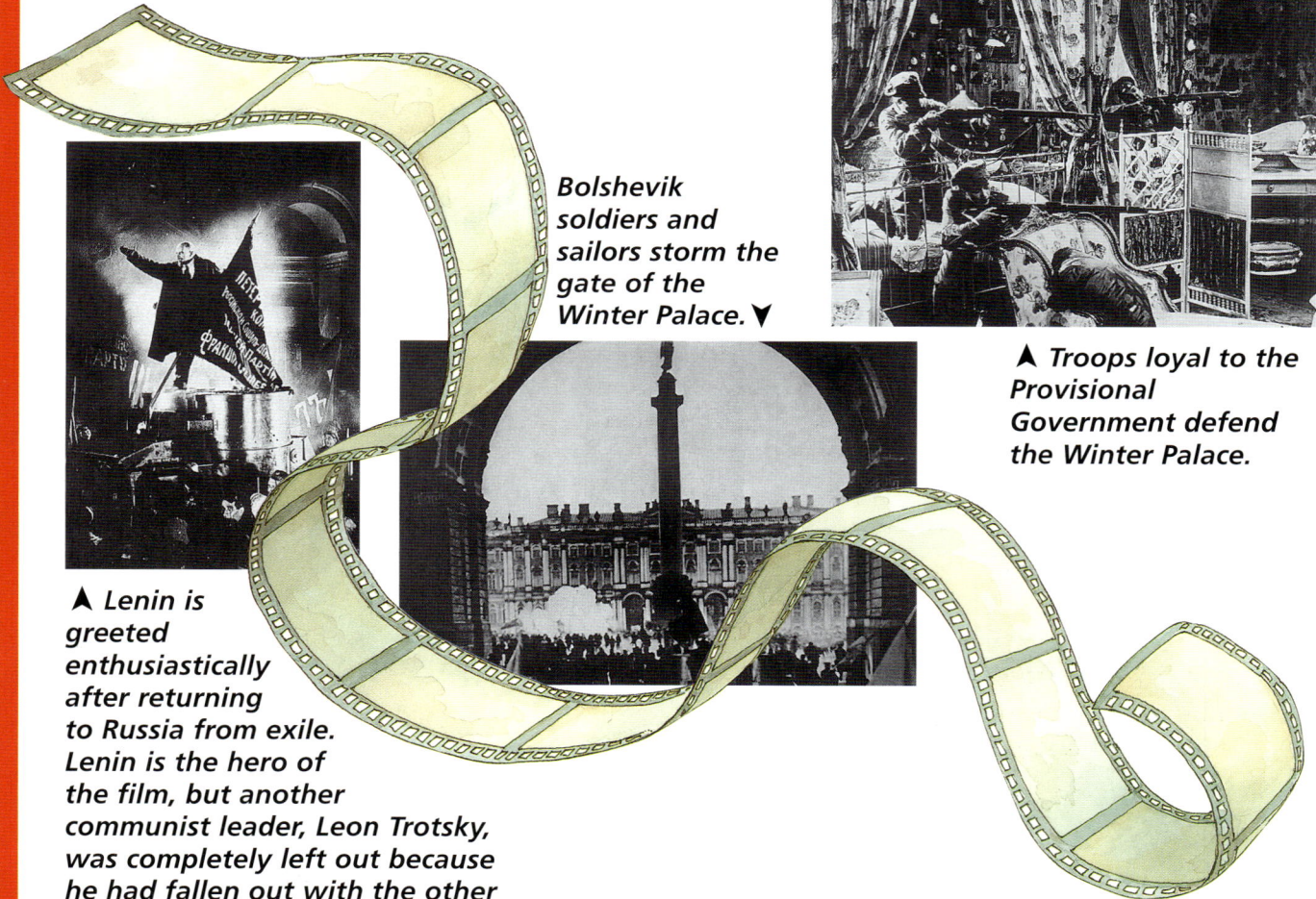

▲ *Lenin is greeted enthusiastically after returning to Russia from exile. Lenin is the hero of the film, but another communist leader, Leon Trotsky, was completely left out because he had fallen out with the other leading communists.*

SOURCE A

Although Lenin was in charge, it was Trotsky who had done most of the planning.

▲ From a recent school textbook.

SOURCE B

The Provisional Government was not overthrown by a mass attack on the Winter Palace. A few Bolsheviks climbed in through a servants' entrance ... and arrested the ministers. Six people, five of them Bolsheviks, were casualties of bad shooting by their own side.

▲ A.J.P. Taylor, from Revolutions and Revolutionaries, 1980.

SOURCE C

... everyone rushed forward shouting 'hurrah'. I was at the front, I ran up the stairs and stumbled into a big hall where there was a detachment of officer cadets with their rifles at the ready. I shouted to the defenders, 'Throw down your rifles!' and they threw down their weapons as if to order. They'd seen how angry we were.

▲ Alexander Brianski, one of the Bolsheviks who took part in the attack.

SOURCE D

According to this morning's information the battle was fairly heated ... It is impossible to know the casualty figures. Three hundred women soldiers are said to have been killed, but this figure seems to me exaggerated.

▲ A French diplomat's account of the storming of the Winter Palace, written the day after it happened.

SOURCE E

What happened to the Women's Battalion? we asked a Bolshevik officer. 'Oh – the women!' he laughed. 'They were all huddled up in a back room. We had a terrible time deciding what to do with them – many were in hysterics and so on. So we finally marched them to the train station and sent them back to their camp.'

▲ John Reed, from Ten days that Shook the World, 1926. Reed was an American eyewitness who sympathised with the Bolsheviks.

INVESTIGATION

You are the investigator!

You can now write your report.

For each of the three still pictures of Eisenstein's film, explain the following:

■ What does the still suggest about the events of 1917?

■ In what way do the sources disagree with the picture?

■ What changes would you ask the producer to make to his film version of October?

Conclude by saying:

■ Why you think Sergei Eisenstein's film is inaccurate;

■ Whether you think a truthful version of the events would make a good film.

6 HOW DID COMMUNISM CHANGE RUSSIA?

THIS CHAPTER ASKS
How were the Russian people affected by Communism?
How did Stalin control the Soviet Union?

NEW WORDS

COLLECTIVISATION: government takeover of all farmland.
DICTATOR: a single person who holds all political power.
PURGES: a time when Stalin punished everyone he did not trust.
SOVIET UNION: new name for Russia after 1922.

THE RISE OF STALIN

Lenin died in 1924, and after a brief struggle between the other leading communists, he was replaced as leader by Joseph Stalin.

RUSSIA TRANSFORMED

Stalin realised that if the **Soviet Union** was to survive as the world's only communist country, it would have to become modern and strong. In 1929 he set out to modernise the country's agriculture. By a process called **collectivisation** all the farmland was taken from the peasants, who were paid a small wage and made to work for the government. Many peasants hated losing their land, but Stalin used great brutality against them. Those who resisted were accused of being kulaks (wealthy greedy peasants) and were sent to prison camps where millions of them died of cold and hunger.

Stalin was also determined to build up Soviet industry. In 1928 he started a series of Five Year Plans which set targets that every factory had to meet within five years. Workers and managers who failed to meet their targets were imprisoned or shot, but those who worked hard were often paid more than everyone else. Stalin's use of harsh punishments and rewards meant that production of important goods like steel, coal and iron soared. The Soviet Union was transformed into one of the most powerful industrial countries in the world.

SOURCE A

▲ *A communist poster showing how a foreign capitalist who laughs at the Five Year Plans in 1928, is silenced by Soviet industrial success five years later.*

SOURCE B

▲ *A mass grave of people who were shot on Stalin's orders. Investigators opened the grave in 1989.*

POLITICAL CHANGES

The Bolsheviks had always been willing to use violence when they thought it necessary, but Stalin became a **dictator** by using brutality and fear as a normal part of government policy. From 1934 onwards, he used a series of **purges** to deal with everyone suspected of plotting against him. All the leading party members were killed, along with more than half of the officers in the army. Even the leaders of the secret police, the NKVD, were shot for not shooting enough people! Over one million minor party members joined the kulaks in newly built prison camps, known as the gulags, where perhaps as many as 12 million people died from cold, over-work and hunger.

In order to hide his brutality, Stalin launched a big propaganda campaign which showed him as a kind and ingenious leader who worked hard for his people. In 1936 he even said that people could express their opinions in free elections. Of course only one political party was allowed and Stalin made sure that he kept all power for himself. The Soviet Union was now a much more powerful country, but its people were not free or equal as Marx had intended.

A Russian joke.
'Did you hear about the burglary at the Parliament building?'
'Next year's election results were stolen.'

Q **1.** For each of the people listed below explain what life might have been like before the changes, how the changes might have affected them and how they might have felt.

■ A Kulak who owns a prosperous farm
■ The manager of a factory which is failing to meet its targets
■ A hard-working factory worker
■ An old Bolshevik who fought alongside Lenin to overthrow the Tsar and create Communism in Russia
■ A foreign capitalist.

2. You are a police inspector trying to identify the bodies in **Source B**. Use the text and the sources in this chapter to compile a list of the type of people who might be in the grave.

Showing the real Joseph Stalin

YOUR MISSION: to discover the real face of Joseph Stalin.

A Russian historian visited an exhibition of paintings produced during the time of Stalin. As she looked at each painting she became more and more angry. She remembered many of the sources which she had studied during her own research into the period. These sources strongly disagreed with the image of Stalin shown in the paintings. Look carefully at the paintings below and examine the historian's thoughts.

'Stalin is too rude and although we communists might put up with this, it is hardly what we would expect from a leader of the Party. That is why I suggest he should be removed from his post.'

▲ **Lenin writing about Stalin in 1923.**

▲ **Painting 1. Stalin helps Lenin to lead the Revolution.**

▲ **A starving child during 1929–32.**

▲ **Painting 2. Stalin on a modern collective farm.**

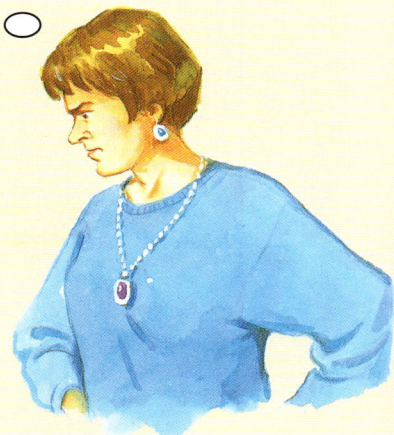

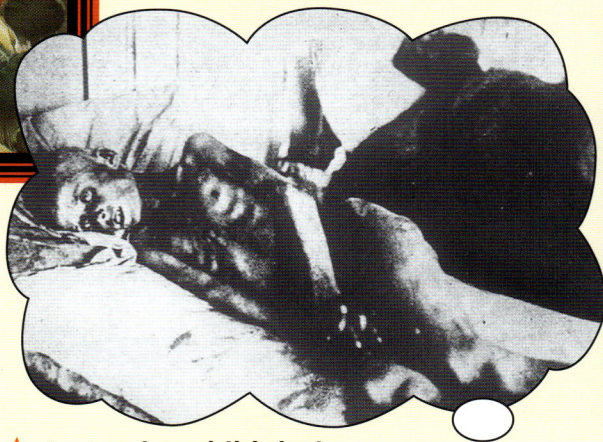

▲ Painting 3. Stalin meets the ordinary Soviet people.

'No one feels safe in the Soviet Union. No one, as he goes to bed, knows whether he will escape arrest in the night .... You have forced those who go along with you to walk with disgust through pools of their own comrades' blood.'

▲ A letter written by a Communist in 1939.

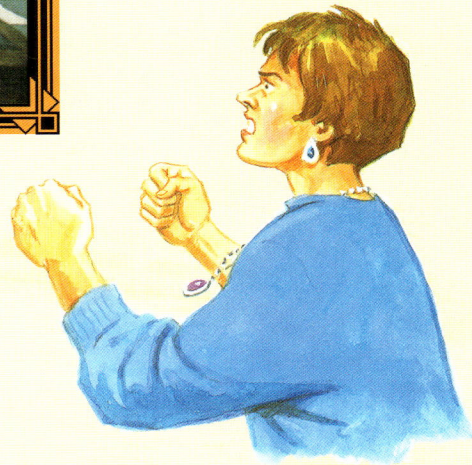

INVESTIGATION

You are the investigator!

1. Look carefully at these pages again. Then complete the table below by referring closely to each painting and the historian's thoughts.

What is the artist saying about Stalin and how does the painting make Stalin look good?	Why does the historian disagree with the artist?
Painting 1	
Painting 2	
Painting 3	

2. The historian decided to write a letter to the art gallery's curator. Use your table to write this letter. Write one paragraph about what each painting seems to be saying and how the historian feels about this. Then finish the letter with a paragraph which explains how she feels the exhibition should be changed.

7 THE END OF GERMAN DEMOCRACY

THIS CHAPTER ASKS
How did Hitler destroy German democracy?
How did Nazi rule affect the lives of the German people?

PROBLEMS FOR THE NEW GERMAN GOVERNMENT

After World War One Germany became a democracy with a new government known as the Weimar **Republic**. Not everyone welcomed democracy, however. Many people blamed the government for the harsh terms of the Treaty of Versailles and demanded revenge against the Allies. Others, who thought that the new government didn't do enough for the poor, wanted to overthrow democracy and replace the government with a Communist regime.

Democracy in Germany was undermined by a terrible economic situation because the government had to meet the cost of the war and pay huge reparations to the Allies. They could only manage to do this by printing more and more money, but this meant that the money was worth much less as prices rose. Many people found that their savings were made worthless by this **inflation**.

SOURCE A

Everything went black before my eyes as I staggered back to my ward and buried my aching head between blankets and pillow.... the following days were terrible to bear, and the nights worse. During the nights my hatred increased for the people who did this terrible crime.

▲ *How a young soldier named Adolf Hitler reacted to the news of the ceasefire.*

SOURCE B

▲ *Hitler was a great public speaker. Look carefully at the reactions of his audience in this painting of an early Nazi meeting.*

During the early 1920s German money became almost worthless because of inflation. In November 1923 a loaf of bread might cost as much as half a million pounds!

**Adolf Hitler
1899–1945**

Born in a small town in Austria, Hitler dropped out of school and moved to Vienna. He thought himself a great artist but he could not get a place at art college. He lived as a tramp until 1914 when he joined the German Army. During World War One he was decorated for bravery.

▲ *Some businessmen feared the Communists who would take away their wealth. As this poster shows, they gave money to Hitler.*

THE THREAT FROM ADOLF HITLER

In 1919 an ex-army corporal named Adolf Hitler joined a small political party in Munich. He soon rose to be its leader and changed its name to the Nazi Party. The group was only one of many small parties at the time who expressed a hatred for democracy and a desire for revenge on Germany's foreign enemies. In 1923 he tried to seize power but he failed and was briefly imprisoned.

HITLER'S IDEAS

Hitler used his nine months in prison to write down his ideas in a book which he called *Mein Kampf* (My Struggle). He blamed the Jews for Germany's defeat in the war and the economic problems which followed. He said that they should be punished and that Germany must regain its position as a world power. Together these two ideas took away German responsibility for their own misfortunes and offered a hopeful future. Germany depended heavily on loans from the USA, but when the American economy crashed in 1929 these loans were withdrawn, leaving the German economy in real trouble. In this situation many people were willing to listen to Hitler's ideas.

Six million Germans were unemployed and many of them turned to Communism as a way out of their desperate situation. To many others it seemed that Hitler was the only man capable of stopping the Communists. He posed as a respectable politician with popular policies like a promise to cut unemployment – but he also used his brutal supporters, called the SA (or stormtroopers), to beat up any opposition. His tactics worked. In 1933 he was made Chancellor and he was able to use his position to pass the Enabling Act. This gave Hitler the right to make laws. In July 1933 he used this power to ban all other political parties. German democracy was at an end.

Q **1.** Explain why the following people might have lost confidence in democracy and how they could be persuaded to support the Nazis:

■ An unemployed worker
■ A disabled ex-soldier
■ A wealthy businessman.

2. Use your three answers to make a speech for Hitler attacking the Weimar Republic and describing his own ideas.

A better life under the Nazis?

HITLER TAKES CONTROL

Hitler made himself undisputed leader or *Führer* of a Germany in which the Nazis were the only legal political party. But he sought more than political control of the country; his regime was totalitarian. This means that it aimed to completely dominate and transform the lives of ordinary Germans. Did the Nazis achieve this aim? How were the German people affected by Hitler's policies?

WORKERS IN NAZI GERMANY

As soon as he came to power Hitler quickly reduced unemployment by putting thousands to work on government building projects. His decision to rebuild Germany's armed forces meant that unemployed men could be absorbed into the army and many more people were found work in the factories which made the new weapons. The unemployment figures fell even further when women and Jews (who did not count in the statistics) were sacked and replaced by registered unemployed.

SOURCE A

Most of those employed on building sites under the public works schemes worked long hours, in primitive conditions, for wages hardly in excess of their previous dole-payments.

▲ *From Purnell's* History of the 20th Century.

It was not all good news for the workers. Unions and strikes were banned and through an organisation known as the RAD the Nazis controlled workers' pay and conditions. Some historians have even argued that only the big employers really benefitted from Nazi rule. They gained huge government contracts on public works and rearmament and they had a strictly controlled workforce which was forced to accept modest pay rises, longer working hours and poorer conditions.

SOURCE B

REICHSAUTOBAHNEN IN DEUTSCHLAND

▲ A poster showing a new German motorway built by a Nazi work scheme.

SOURCE C

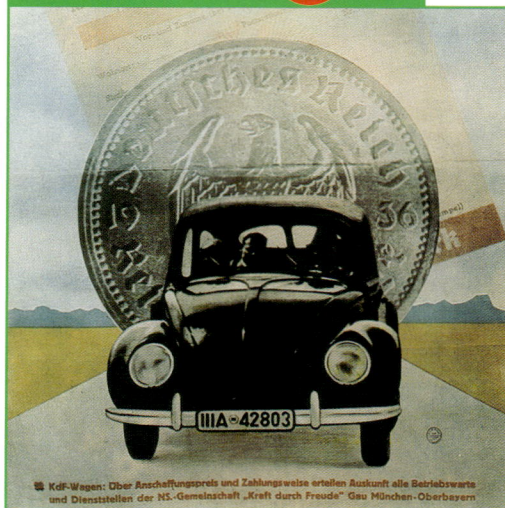

▲ A poster asking workers to save for a car. No workers managed to get one because none were made before the war.

CHILDREN IN NAZI GERMANY

Hitler made a special effort to win children over to Nazism. He believed that German boys must be toughened for the army and girls should be prepared for motherhood. Physical fitness was therefore vital for both boys and girls but it was also important that they should be taught to be loyal Nazis. He thought that schools could serve this purpose and he made sure that all school teachers had to be members of the Nazi Party so that they could teach Nazi ideas.

Many German women fancied Hitler. Hundreds offered to have his baby and two killed themselves out of love for him!

SOURCE D

▲ *School children give the Nazi salute to their teachers.*

Outside school hours boys had to join the Hitler Youth Movement which developed toughness through outdoor pursuits and even gave rifle training to older members. Girls were urged to join the League of German Maidens where they learned domestic skills and were encouraged to look on themselves as future mothers.

WOMEN IN NAZI GERMANY

Hitler believed that the only real role for a woman was in the home as a housewife and mother. So he made sure that many women teachers, doctors, lecturers and civil servants lost their jobs. They were told to stay at home and have children. To help them do this the Nazis provided all sorts of loans and financial gifts for large families. There was even a medal for women who had eight children or more.

Women reacted in different ways to these policies; some may have welcomed them, but others were horrified at the loss of freedom and opportunity.

SOURCE E

When an opponent says, 'I will not come over to your side', I will calmly say, 'Your child belongs to us already ... you will pass on. Your descendants will be Nazis.'

▲ *From a speech by Hitler in 1933.*

Q

1. Look at Sources A, B and C. What do you think a worker's attitude to these three sources might be?

2. Why do you think Sources B and C were produced?

3. Imagine that you are either a boy or a girl growing up in Nazi Germany. Write a letter to a foreign pen pal describing the good and the bad points about:

■ Your current experience as a child;

■ What you expect life to be like when you grow up to be an adult man or woman.

Finish by saying whether you think life is better under the Nazis. Explain your decision.

How did the Nazis control Germany?

NAZI METHODS

The Nazis tried to control every aspect of German life. Those who did not fit in with Nazi ideas had to be punished, but the majority of people were to be persuaded by a massive propaganda campaign organised by Joseph Goebbels. His view of propaganda is summed up in his own words: 'If you tell a lie, tell a big lie'. Below are three of Goebbels's big lies.

> Hitler didn't drink alcohol or smoke tobacco. He was a vegetarian who hated cruelty to animals. He loved his Mum.

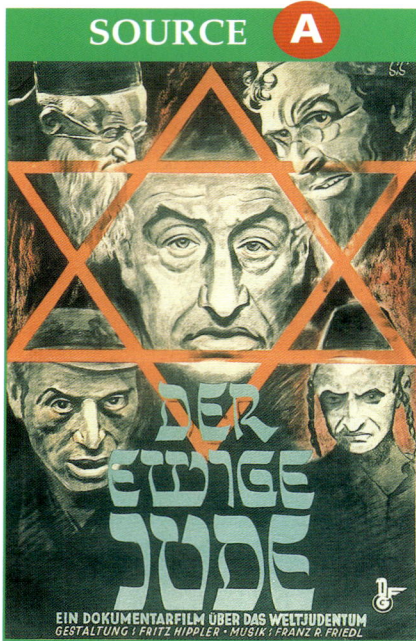

SOURCE A

▲ A poster for the Nazi feature film, The Eternal Jew.

LIE ONE. The Jews were responsible for everything bad which had happened to Germany. They lured Germany into World War One and ensured its defeat. They were behind the Treaty of Versailles and the economic problems of the 1920s. They were the big businessmen who threatened small German shopkeepers but they were also the Communists who threatened big business!

SOURCE B

▲ An ideal Aryan family painted by a Nazi artist.

LIE TWO. The Germans were the master race who were destined to overcome many of the inferior races. The true German or Aryan was physically perfect with blonde hair and blue eyes. Other peoples like the Slavs (East Europeans) were inferior but the Jews were not even classed as human.

SOURCE C

▲ Newsreel footage of Hitler addressing a Nazi rally.

LIE THREE. Hitler was the superhuman saviour of Germany who was always right. It was the duty of every good German to obey the orders of their leader without question.

WHY DID PEOPLE FEAR THE NAZIS?

Many Germans saw through Goebbels's lies but they were often too frightened to defy the Nazis. Opposing political parties quietly closed themselves down, and their leaders fled abroad. The churches might have opposed Nazi brutality but most of them simply decided to co-operate. Courageous individuals who stood out against the Nazis for political or religious reasons soon found themselves victims of Nazi 'justice'.

Hitler's special secret police, the Gestapo, used a system of spies and informers to root out all opposition. Once arrested, the victim could be tortured, imprisoned or even murdered by the Gestapo, who did not have to obey normal laws. Even if an opponent did get to court, Hitler made sure that they would get little sympathy; all the judges were Nazis and during the first six years of Hitler's rule over 500 people were legally executed for 'political offences'.

'PURIFYING' GERMANY

Hitler believed that he had a mission to purify the Aryan race by weeding out the weak, the disabled and the unsuitable. Many different people who did not suit his idea of the ideal German soon became victims of the Gestapo. Jews, Gypsies, homosexuals, criminals and the homeless soon joined the Nazis' political and religious opponents in a newly-built series of prison camps, where they were put to work and treated harshly by brutal guards

SOURCE D

Deutsches Jugendfest
SONNABEND DEN 23. JUNI 1934

FÖRDERT DIE DEUTSCHE JUGEND
DURCH DEN KAUF DES FESTABZEICHENS

▲ *Hitler Youth burn anti-Nazi books. No one who disagreed with the Nazis was allowed to express their views in any form.*

SOURCE E

… whipping, frequent kicking (abdomen or groin), slaps in the face, shooting or wounding with the bayonet … prisoners were forced to stare for hours into glaring lights.

▲ *An account of torture used in the concentration camps.* The Informed Heart, *by B. Bettelheim, 1960.*

Q In **Sources A**, **B** and **C**, Goebbels uses a variety of methods to carry his propaganda (posters, films etc).

1. List all the methods used.

2. Which one do you think would be most effective based on:

■ Numbers reached by the propaganda

■ Most lasting impact

■ The subtlety of the propaganda. Remember propaganda is sometimes more effective if the audience does not realise that it is seeing propaganda.

3. 'These sources are propaganda, so they are of no use to a historian.' Do you agree? Explain your answer.

Hitler's war?

INVESTIGATION

YOUR MISSION: to discover and report on Hitler's intentions.

You are an adviser to the British Prime Minister, Neville Chamberlain. He wants to know whether Hitler intends to go to war and if he does, is Britain likely to be attacked? You must examine the sources and deliver your conclusions in a written report.

Between 1933 and 1939 Hitler adopted a very aggressive foreign policy which overturned the terms of Versailles and expanded German territory. The British Government was so eager to avoid a war that it did nothing to stop him. In September 1939 Hitler went too far; he invaded Poland, and France and Britain finally declared war on Germany. Is it possible that things could have turned out differently? Had the British government understood Hitler better could it have avoided war?

SOURCE A

War is the most natural and most ordinary thing. War is constant; war is everywhere. There is no beginning, there is no conclusion of peace. War is life. All struggle is war.

▲ **Hitler's attitude to war and violence from his biography** Mein Kampf **which was written in 1924, long before he came to power.**

SOURCE B

Germany would be ready to disband her whole military establishment and destroy the small amount of arms she had, if neighbouring countries would do the same.

▲ **Hitler in a speech from 1933 before Germany had built up its armed forces.**

SOURCE C

| 1933: 3 | 1937: 8 | 1939: 37 |

▲ **German defence spending in millions of marks.**

SOURCE D

▲ **Competitors at a Nazi sports day held in 1935, four years before the outbreak of war.**

SOURCE E

We are only safe against the Communists if we have armaments which they respect.

▲ *Hitler speaking to British politicians in 1935.*

SOURCE F

The German population is increasing by 900,000 a year. We need to get new land for our excess population … When we speak of new land, we Nazis mean Russia …

▲ *Hitler writing in* **Mein Kampf,** *1924.*

SOURCE G

'Do you seriously intend to fight the West?' I asked. Hitler stopped and looked at me. 'What else do you think we're arming for?' he retorted. 'We must proceed step by step so that no one will impede our advance. How to do this I don't know yet. But that it will be done is guaranteed by Britain's lack of firmness …

▲ *H. Rauschning, from* **Hitler Speaks.** *Rauschning was a Nazi supporter who fell out with Hitler. When he wrote this book in 1939, he was living in England.*

Hitler wanted the other powers to believe that Germany was well armed. A visiting French politician was taken to an airfield and shown the entire German airforce. Whilst he was driven to another airfield the planes which he had already seen took off and arrived before him so that he was made to think that Germany had twice as many planes than they actually did!

INVESTIGATION

You are the investigator!

Complete the following table. You must consider the reliability of each source. This means looking at the context in which the event or speech took place. What does the event really mean? Might the speaker be telling lies in order to fool his audience or win support? When you have selected the most reliable sources you must use them to reach your conclusions, which will form the basis of your written advice to Chamberlain.

	What does the source say about Hitler's intentions?	How reliable is the source?	Conclusion 1. What is Hitler's attitude to war?
Source A			
Source B			
Source C			
Source D			
Source E			Conclusion 2. Who will he attack?
Source F			
Source G			

8 THE SURVIVAL OF DEMOCRACY

THIS CHAPTER ASKS

What problems did Britain and the USA face between the wars?

Why did democracy survive in these countries?

NEW WORDS

GENERAL STRIKE: a strike joined by many workers in many different industries.

OVER-PRODUCTION: when more goods are produced than can be sold.

WORLD PROBLEMS AFTER WORLD WAR ONE

During the war most governments kept up the effort of their people by promising them better lives when peace came. But for both winners and losers the end of the war brought great hardship and disappointment. The enormous cost of the fighting drained away wealth and left many states with severe economic problems throughout the 1920s. These problems were eased by American loans, but when the American economy began to fail in 1929 nothing could save the people of Europe from hopeless poverty and unemployment.

In such a desperate situation many people came to feel that capitalism and democracy had let them down. They looked for a new way out of their problems. Some saw the enormous success of Stalin's Five Year Plans in the Soviet Union and demanded a Communist revolution in their own countries. Others, especially in the losing states, thought that the overthrow of democracy by a powerful dictator might make things better. They sought to copy the methods of Mussolini in Italy and Hitler in Germany and so, by the mid-1930s much of Europe was ruled by dictators.

It seemed like democracy across the entire world was doomed. Britain and the USA remained important democracies, but they too had real problems. How long could they hold out against the tide of dictatorship? How could they solve their problems and keep democracy alive?

SOURCE A

▲ The Italian dictator, Mussolini, whose Fascist Party overthrew the Italian Parliament in 1922. He was admired by many people outside Italy for tackling unemployment.

SOURCE B

▲ Oswald Mosley, leader of the British Union of Fascists, takes a salute from his supporters. Mosley admired Mussolini but his own party never had more than a few thousand supporters and quickly declined after the mid-1930s.

SOURCE C

▲ Unemployed workers from Jarrow in the North East of England march to London in 1936. This was one of many peaceful protest marches.

When the Jarrow workers returned from their protest march against unemployment, they had their dole money cut because they weren't available for work!

BRITAIN BETWEEN THE WARS

With the end of the war the British economy ran into difficulties. The government had promised much better homes and employment for British workers, but it soon found that it was impossible to pay for these things. Instead, the government cut back on spending, leaving many British workers to a life of squalor and hopeless unemployment.

OPPOSITION TO THE GOVERNMENT

British workers were well organised in trades unions and they tried to use strike action to protect themselves from wage cuts and unemployment. In 1926 the miners went on strike to prevent the mine owners from cutting their wages. They were supported by workers from many other industries, and it may have seemed to some people that the country was near to a worker's take-over. The **General Strike** all but ended after less than two weeks because many of the union leaders had no desire to take political action; they simply wanted to safeguard their workers. Most British workers didn't want violent action, instead they hoped that the Labour Party could bring about peaceful democratic change. The more extreme British Communist Party never had more than one MP throughout this period.

SOURCE D

▲ Workers fight with police during the General Strike in this painting from 1953. In reality there was very little violence during the strike.

THE BIG PICTURE

SOURCE E

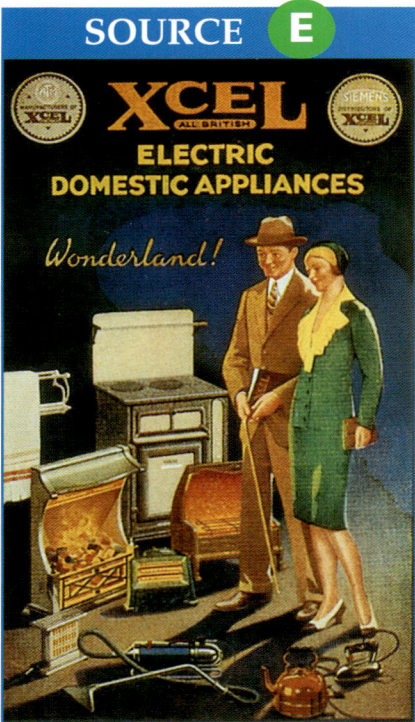

▲ *An advertisement from the 1920s showing many of the electrical appliances made by the newer British industries.*

THE MYTH OF THE DEPRESSION

Although many British workers faced long-term unemployment and poverty during the 1920s and 1930s many more actually saw a rise in their standard of living. Those who suffered worked in older heavy industries like mining and ship-building, based in the North of England, Scotland and Wales. These industries found it impossible to compete with foreign competition which used newer machinery and better working practices to undercut their prices.

In the Midlands and the South-East, workers who made cars and new electrical products experienced much less unemployment and had higher wages. They were able to afford many of the luxuries which they produced and some could even buy new homes in the suburbs away from the old inner-city slums. Perhaps this is the most significant reason why democracy in Britain never really came under threat. Many workers were doing well and did not want to change their system of government.

THE USA IN THE 1920s

The USA emerged from the war to an economic boom. American factories had pioneered new production techniques which made goods affordable to a wide range of people. For the first time ever many ordinary people could afford luxuries like cars, fridges, and radios.

Profitable factories meant well-paid workers who spent more and more money on factory products. During the 1920s the American economy boomed as many people spent as much as they could. But in 1929 a sudden slump, known as the Wall Street Crash, led to serious economic problems. Millions of ordinary people experienced mass unemployment and despair in the richest country in the world.

SOURCE F

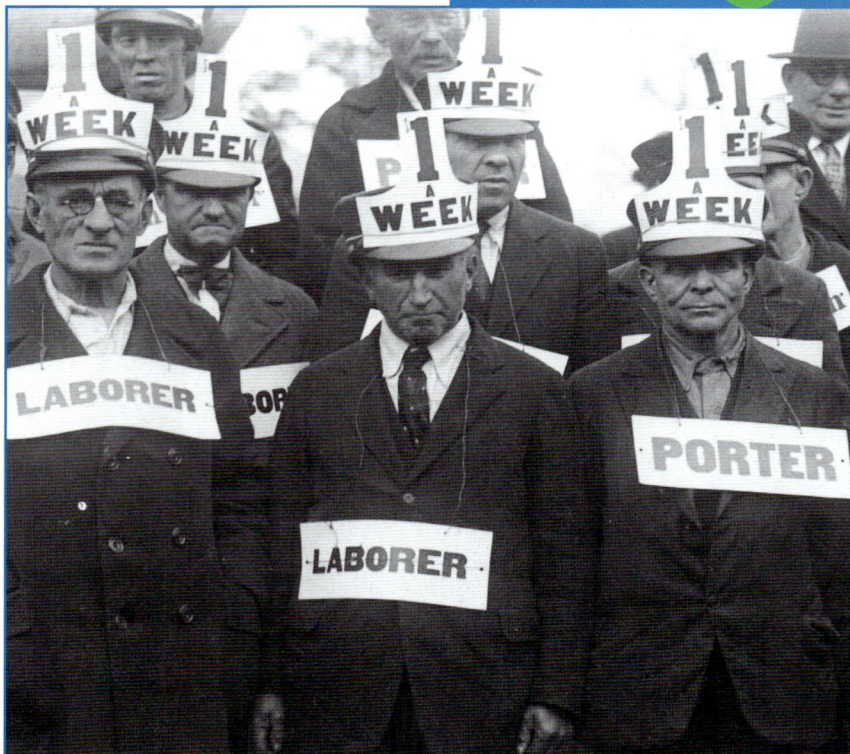

◀ *Desperate unemployed American workers offer to work for one dollar a week.*

WHY WAS THERE A DEPRESSION IN THE USA?

American factories were able to turn out a record amount of goods using the new techniques, but many Americans were too poor to afford these products and the factories could hardly sell them to impoverished European countries. The result was **over-production**; unsold goods piled up in factory storerooms, profits fell and workers lost their jobs as factory owners tried to balance their books.

THE USA AND THE DEPRESSION

By 1932 there were more than twelve million Americans without work and, as there was no system of unemployment benefit, they were forced to beg or rely on free food handouts from charities. Those who could no longer afford to pay their rent found themselves homeless. In the summer of 1932 unemployed ex-soldiers marched to Washington to demand help from the government, but they were met by the army who fired tear gas to disperse them. Some people believed that the greatest capitalist democracy in the world was about to fall apart.

THE NEW DEAL

In November 1932 America elected Franklin D. Roosevelt as its new President. He promised a New Deal for all Americans and he immediately set about spending huge amounts of government money on a series of job creation schemes to help the unemployed. The schemes did not completely solve the problem of unemployment, but they did give many people some hope and allowed them to feed themselves. Some historians have argued that the assistance and the hope which Roosevelt's New Deal gave to the American people helped to save democracy in America.

Some of the jobs which Roosevelt's government created were of little value. Hundreds of people were employed to walk around the centre of Washington with balloons on very long strings. Why? To scare the birds off public buildings.

SOURCE G

POUR IT ON!

▲ An American war poster from 1941. The depression only really ended in Britain and the USA when both countries had to prepare for war.

Q

1. Why did some people lose faith in democracy after World War One?

2. Why were many areas of Britain prosperous whilst others were poor?

3. Why did the US economy boom in the 1920s?

4. Why did democracy survive in Britain and the USA? Explain by using the following points:

■ The moderate attitudes of British workers and their leaders

■ New industries in Britain

■ President Roosevelt's New Deal.

Black Americans between the wars

INEQUALITY IN THE DEMOCRACIES

Although politicians in democratic countries like Britain and the USA might be quick to point out the failings of the dictatorships, the democracies themselves were far from perfect. Many people living in democratic countries felt unfairly treated.

SOURCE A

▲ A poster showing black American soldiers in World War One. The first two medals awarded to US soldiers went to black Americans. The bearded man in the top right of the picture is President Abraham Lincoln who ended black slavery in the 1860s.

SOURCE B

Many thousands of young black men served in the armed forces during the war, but this brought no escape from discrimination. The marines accepted no black recruits at all and the navy employed them only as cooks and waiters. The army recruited many thousands but placed them in segregated units and took a long time to promote black officers.

▲ From A companion to American Studies, Denis Welland, 1974.

SOURCE C

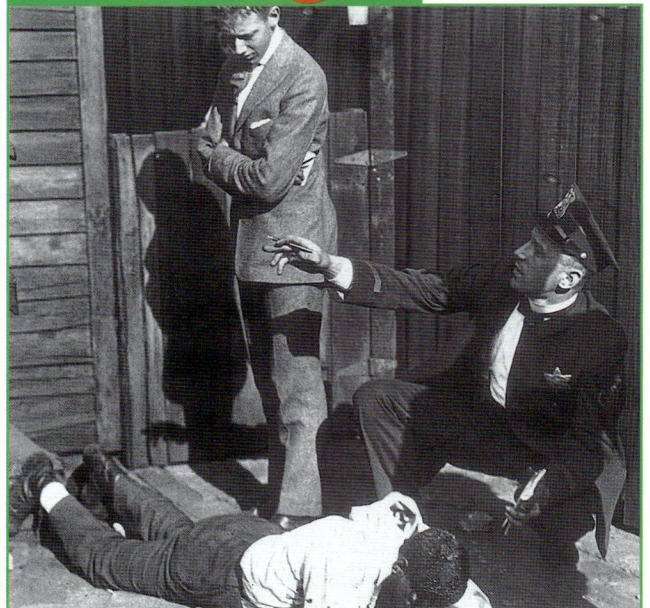

▲ Just after the war a wave of violent race riots swept through northern cities. In this picture an injured black man lies bleeding in the street.

BLACK AMERICANS AND WORLD WAR ONE

During the war many black Americans moved from the poor farms of the South where they faced poverty and discrimination to the large northern cities where there was lots of work in the war industries. They hoped to improve their lives but many found that poverty and prejudice followed them to their new homes.

LIFE IN THE NORTHERN CITIES

Black Americans in the big cities soon found themselves living in the poorest ghetto areas. Poverty and the hostility of white Americans stopped them from moving out to better housing. They also suffered the worst unemployment, usually being the 'last hired and first fired', and even when they could find work it was always doing the least desirable jobs. Meanwhile, local laws prevented their children from attending good schools which were reserved for whites, so it seemed that the next generation of black people had little hope of doing any better than their parents.

THE 'NEW NEGROES' AND BLACK PROTEST

Despite the discrimination, some black Americans did make progress. These 'New Negroes' often lived on the edge of the **ghettos** where they made a good living as shop-keepers, dentists, doctors and lawyers. Their example gave other black people the hope that they too might get out of the ghetto. They led peaceful protest movements which attracted the support of middle-class whites and began to slowly break down the racial barriers in the Northern cities. They could do very little, however, for those black Americans who remained in the South where prejudice was even more severe.

SOURCE D

▲ *A separate entrance for blacks at this cinema kept them apart from other races. After World War One segregation like this was very common.*

SOURCE E

▲ *A black jazz band in the 1920s. Jazz music allowed some black musicians to make a good living. It was popular with many white people.*

Q

1. Consider **Sources A** and **B**. Which one do you think gives the most reliable view of the black US soldier's experience of World War One?

2. Would the soldiers in **Source A** have been surprised by **Sources C** and **D**? Explain your answer using **Source B**.

3. Can **Source E** be used to prove that the USA was less racist after World War One and black Americans were better off?

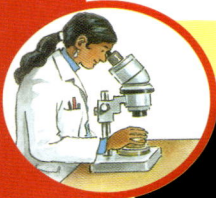

Why was Nancy Astor important?

YOUR MISSION: to discover why it was important for women to be represented in Parliament.

▲ Nancy Astor.

SOURCE A

The first woman to take her seat in the House of Commons was Lady Astor … since that time the number of women MPs has never been large, usually about twenty, and it is difficult to find examples of direct influence on national policy.

▲ From a school textbook written in 1970.

Nancy Astor 1879–1964

Daughter of an American millionaire. married to a British Lord. Played no part in suffragette campaign. Elected to parliament in November 1919.

WOMEN MEETING THE CHALLENGE

Since women first gained the right to vote in 1918 their position in British society and in employment has steadily improved. Women successfully demonstrated that they could do 'men's work' during World War One, but at the end of the war most were forced to leave their jobs so that returning soldiers could be employed. In World War Two women again took over important jobs and this time they managed to keep many of them.

As women proved themselves in the job market it became increasingly difficult for men to deny them equal employment rights. In 1970 the government passed laws forcing employers to pay the same wages to men and women who did the same job. Five years later women were given equal rights to education, jobs and housing. Other government measures such as the introduction of family allowance, nursery education and health provision have also greatly improved women's quality of life.

DID GETTING THE VOTE REALLY MATTER?

Many suffragettes wanted the vote so that they could use it to force the government to act for the benefit of women. They felt that a parliament which did not have to worry about how women voted would never be interested in passing laws to help them. Were they right? Did political influence improve the lives of women?

To answer this we will look at the experience of Nancy Astor, the first woman to sit in parliament.

SOURCE B

It is often thought that the small band of women MPs had little impact in the House of Commons. Yet sixteen Acts protecting women's interests were passed in the early 1920s, ranging from improved maternity services, pensions for widows, divorce on equal grounds to men, better maintainence terms for illegitimate children and separated wives and equal guardianship rights to children.

▲ Angela Holdsworth, from **Out of the Dolls House, 1988.**

SOURCE C

The arrival of the early women MPs dented the masculine world of parliamentary practice and politics. No longer could it simply think about what men wanted. Nancy Astor made history … she changed the whole political debate.

▲ *Sheila Rowbotham, from* **A Century of Women**, *1997.*

SOURCE D

▲ *Young women on their way to vote in the 1929 elections.*

SOURCE E

Milk for poor children.
Help for unmarried mothers.
Pensions for widows.
Job training for unemployed women.
Child abuse.
Women Police.

▲ *The topics on which Lady Astor spoke in parliament during her first three years.*

SOURCE F

… much of the pro-female legislation of the 1920s was about improving women's position as 'wives and mothers' rather than granting them equality, political power or career opportunities.

▲ *Pamela Horn, from* **Women in the 1920s**, *1995.*

INVESTIGATION

You are the investigator!

1. Below are a list of statements about the impact which Nancy Astor had in parliament. Find the source which supports each statement and explain your choice.

- She changed the attitudes of male MPs
- She probably had very little influence
- She helped poorer women and children (two sources)
- Better-off women might have felt that she did not do enough for them.

2. You are an election officer for Nancy Astor and you approach the women in the car (**Source D**) to ask for their vote. Use the sources to explain:

- What Astor has achieved in parliament.
- Why Astor has concentrated on helping poorer women
- Why it is important to have women MPs.

9 WORLD WAR TWO 1939–42

THIS CHAPTER ASKS

Why was Germany so successful in the first half of the war?

What was it like to live through the Blitz?

Read the text for each arrow in the right order.

NEW WORDS

LUFTWAFFE: German airforce.

PANZERS: German tanks.

❷ May and June 1940
The German army launched a two-pronged attack through gaps in the French defensive system. They quickly forced Holland, Belgium and France to surrender by using a new form of warfare called *Blitzkrieg* (lightning war). The demoralised British Army managed to escape back to Britain from Dunkirk, but they left behind all their tanks and heavy weapons.

❶ September 1939 – May 1940
Germany conquered Poland then occupied Denmark. British troops sent to defend Norway were easily defeated. Winston Churchill replaced Neville Chamberlain as Prime Minister.

❸ July to September 1940
In the Battle of Britain the Luftwaffe attempted to destroy the Royal Air Force by constant attacks. Had they succeeded they might have been able to invade Britain. Instead the Luftwaffe suffered heavy losses and in September switched to bombing British cities at night in the hope of making the civilians beg their government for peace. These bombing raids lasted from September 1940 to May 1941 and became known as the Blitz. Britain was kept going by American supplies. In December 1941 America entered the war against Germany.

❹ Germany sent troops to North Africa to help Italy fight Britain. Germany overran Yugoslavia and Greece. British soldiers in Greece escaped to Egypt.

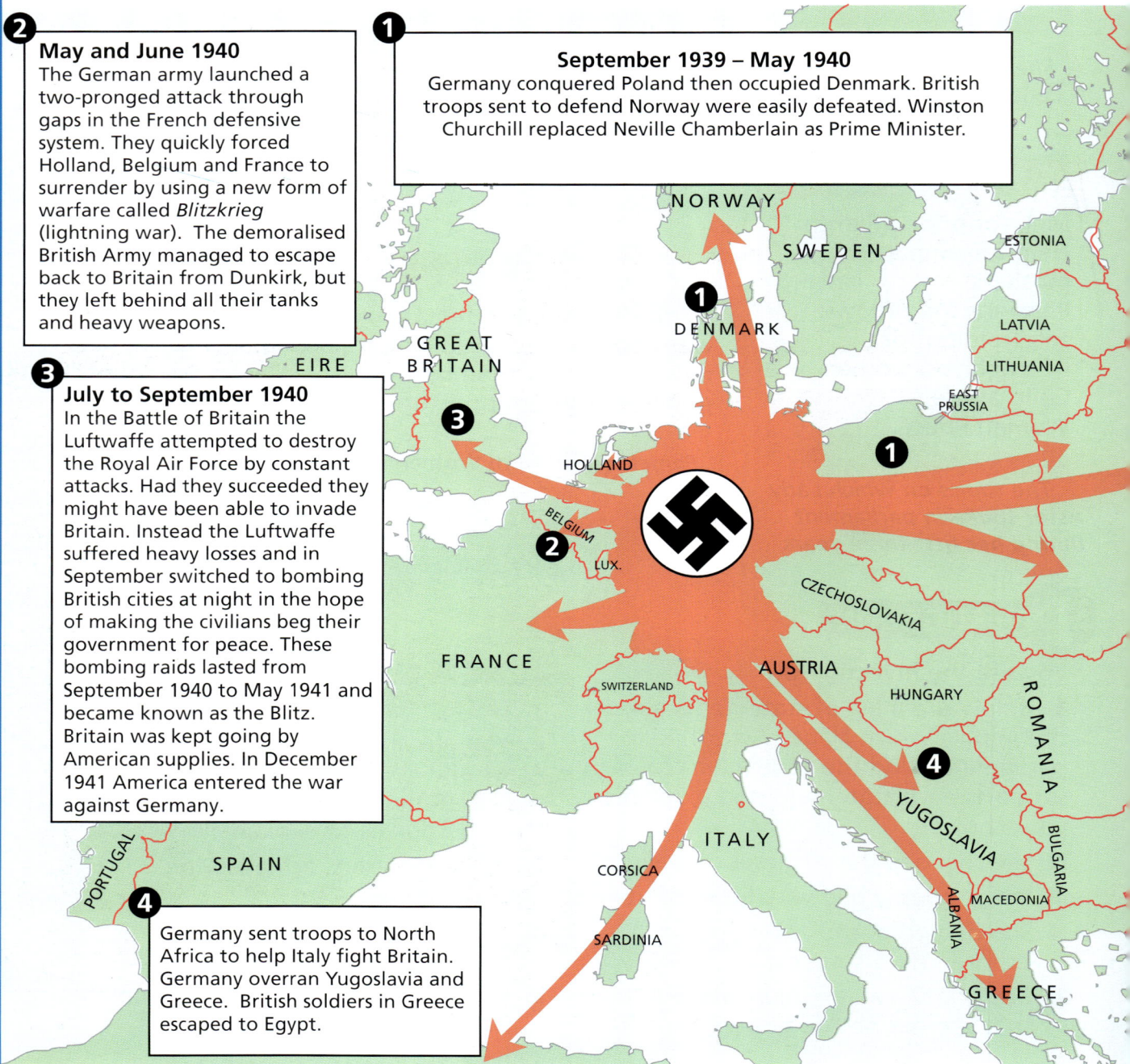

NORWAY

SWEDEN

ESTONIA

DENMARK

LATVIA

GREAT BRITAIN

LITHUANIA

EIRE

EAST PRUSSIA

HOLLAND

BELGIUM

LUX.

CZECHOSLOVAKIA

FRANCE

AUSTRIA

HUNGARY

ROMANIA

SWITZERLAND

YUGOSLAVIA

BULGARIA

ITALY

PORTUGAL

SPAIN

CORSICA

ALBANIA

MACEDONIA

SARDINIA

GREECE

Q

1. Why was Germany unable to defeat Britain?

2. Why do you think the USA's entry into the war might be very important?

3. Make two separate lists of German achievements and failures up to 1942.

4. Would someone at the end of 1942 have thought that Germany was going to win the war? Use the information on your lists to answer the question.

RUSSIA

5

June 1941
Hitler launched a surprise attack on the Soviet Union. At first it was extremely successful, in the first few weeks one million prisoners were taken and over one thousand Soviet aircraft were destroyed on the ground. By December German troops surrounded Leningrad but they could not take it; they had come within sight of Moscow; and (September 1942) they started a vicious house to house battle for Stalingrad.

MOLDAVIA

RUSSIA

TURKEY

Picture 1 *A destroyed German aircraft lies in a field in Southern England.*

Picture 2 *Soviet civilians murdered by the Nazis are identified by their relatives.*

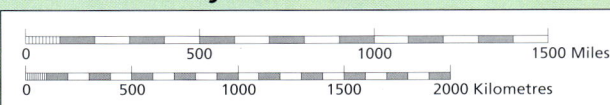

Why was Blitzkrieg so successful?

BRITAIN AND FRANCE PREPARE FOR ATTACK

After the experience of World War One, the French were determined that in any future war German soldiers would be kept out of France and French casualties would be kept to a minimum. They hoped to achieve this by building a sort of super trench with powerful forts known as the Maginot Line along their border with Germany. Once again Britain sent a small army to defend Northern France.

THE FALL OF FRANCE

Most people imagined that there would be another long and costly war like World War One. Instead, when the German attack on France finally came, in May 1940, it lasted only seven weeks and France was forced to surrender at a cost of less than thirty thousand German casualties. Why was France defeated so easily? The answer is *Blitzkrieg* (lightning war), the new German way of making war.

SOURCE A

▲ Aircraft bomb troops on the ground as well as targets to the rear including headquarters, bridges, roads and telephone exchanges.

▲ Paratroops and glider troops are dropped behind enemy lines to capture important positions such as bridges and forts.

▲ Tanks are massed together into Panzer Divisions. They attack at a weak point and cut deep into enemy territory destroying supply and communication systems.

▲ Enemy strong-points are cut off without supplies. The Panzer Divisions are closely followed by infantry in trucks.

▲ How Blitzkrieg worked. Pictures from modern war comics.

THE GERMAN ATTACK

On 10 May 1940 a surprise German attack though the Ardennes completely by-passed the Maginot Line. The Allies had thought that the Ardennes was too rugged to allow tanks through, so the Panzer divisions encountered only light resistance from the startled defenders.

German tanks now pushed deep into French territory cutting the defenders in two and throwing their plans into chaos. When the Germans reached the channel ports the British government feared that their army would be cut off without a means of retreat, so orders were given for an evacuation through Dunkirk. Over 300,000 men were taken back to Britain before the surrounding German forces could close in. France fought on until 22 June, when it was forced to sign a cease fire and agree to German peace terms.

> The Treaty of Versailles would not allow the German army to have any armoured vehicles, so during the 1920s they practised with huge cardboard cut-out tanks.

SOURCE C

The French forces were badly equipped, badly trained and badly led. They had not been modernised after the First World War …

▲ *From* Total War*.*

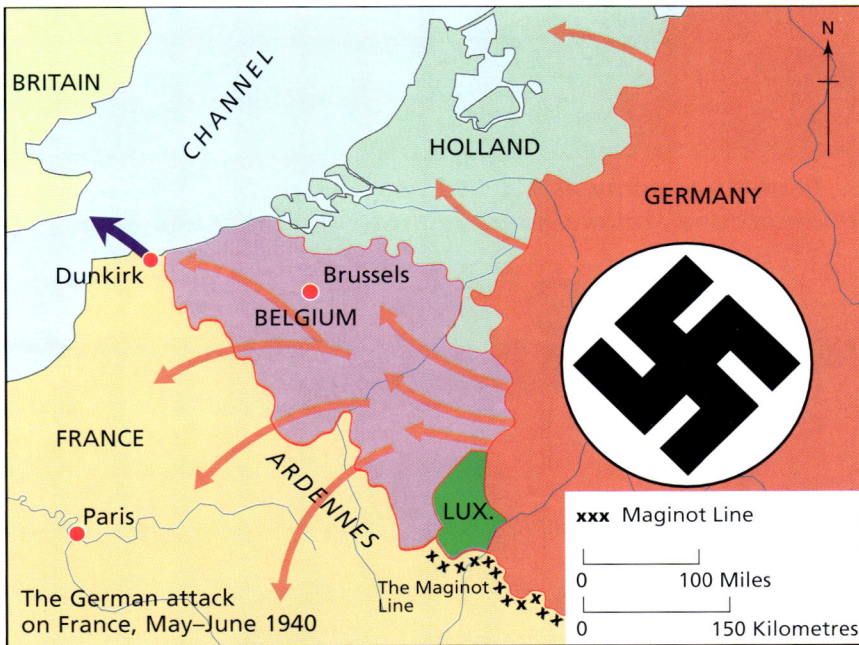

The German attack on France, May–June 1940

xxx Maginot Line

0   100 Miles

0   150 Kilometres

SOURCE B

The battle of France was won by superior skill and not by crushing weight of numbers. In the vital department of tanks the Germans were numerically weaker with some 2,700 against nearly 3,000 French and 200 British. The quality of the tanks on the two sides was about the same. But in tactics and leadership the French and British were outclassed.

▲ *Peter Calvocoressi and Guy Wint, from* Total War*, 1972.*

Q

1. The pictures in **Source A** are from modern comics. How useful are they to a historian describing German military methods?

Answer the question by considering each in turn without looking at the captions. What exactly can you find out?

2. Look carefully at the map. Why was the Maginot Line an expensive failure?

3. Do **Sources B** and **C** agree or disagree about the reason for French defeat?

4. Compare Haig's plan for the attack on the Somme on page 22 with German *Blitzkrieg*. Explain how new technology made the two attacks so different.

How did people get through the Blitz?

YOUR MISSION: to discover the effects of the Blitz on the British people.

65,000 British and 600,000 German civilians were killed by bombing between 1939 and 1945.

THE BLITZ

In September 1940 the Luftwaffe began a series of night raids on British cities. At first they targeted London, but from mid-November onwards they bombed many other cities. The Blitz, which lasted until May 1941, caused terrible destruction. Over 40,000 people were killed, 86,000 were seriously wounded and it is estimated that as many as one and a half million people were made homeless. Despite the suffering, most British people were willing to fight on.

SOURCE A

▲ Perhaps as many as 160,000 people crowded into London underground stations every night to avoid the bombing.

SOURCE B

The first time I went there, I had to come out, I felt sick. You couldn't see anything, you could just smell the overwhelming stench … There were thousands and thousands of people lying head to toe, all along the bays with no facilities. At the beginning there were only four earth buckets down the far end for toilets.

▲ A visitor describes conditions at Tilbury railway arches where up to 16,000 people sheltered every night.

SOURCE C

▲ A family Anderson shelter. One and a half million of these do-it-yourself shelters were delivered to Londoners.

SOURCE D

It became a grim and ghastly satisfaction when a body was fairly constructed – but if one was too lavish in making one body almost whole, then another would have sad gaps. There were always odd members which didn't seem to fit and there were too many legs.

▲ *A woman volunteer describes how she prepared bomb victims for burial.*

The government expected heavy civilian casualties. They ordered hundreds of thousands of coffins in advance but as there was not enough wood they had to be made out of papier mâché.

SOURCE E

They stormed at you as soon as you got out of the car with cries of 'It was good of you to come Winnie. We thought you'd come. We can take it. Give it 'em back …' Churchill promised to get complete revenge.

▲ *How Londoners reacted to a visit from Churchill, described by his military adviser.*

SOURCE F

▲ *A woman is rescued from the rubble of her house. Incredibly, she survived.*

SOURCE G

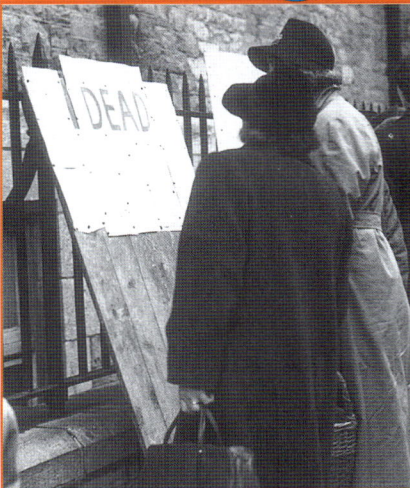

▲ *How the people of Plymouth discovered who had been killed on the morning after a raid.*

INVESTIGATION

You are the investigator!

You are a Home Office official who has been sent to report on the effects of the Blitz. The Home Office has set you a number of questions which you must answer in your report. Look at each of the sources carefully, they will help you with the answers.

■ It is estimated that six out of every ten people stay at home during raids. Why is this? How can they be encouraged to take shelter?

■ How do you feel that we could improve the way we deal with the dead and inform their relatives?

■ What arrangements will be necessary for helping homeless survivors?

■ Should the public be informed about our own bombing raids on Germany?

■ Do you think that the public are willing to fight on?

57

10 WORLD WAR TWO 1942–45

THIS CHAPTER ASKS

Why did the war turn against Germany?
Why could the Nazis not defeat the
Soviet Union?
What made D-Day a success?
Why did the USA use atomic weapons
on Japan?

Read the text for each arrow in the right
order.

Picture 1. *American bombers being shot down over Germany.*

1 1942 to 1945
British and American aircraft
bombed industrial targets in
Germany but they also deliberately
flattened whole cities like Hamburg
(July 1943) and Dresden (July 1945)
killing thousands of German
civilians. Long-range Allied fighters
virtually destroyed the Luftwaffe
over Germany, making a cross-
channel invasion possible without
any danger from the air by 1944.

2 On 6 June 1944 a huge army of Allied
troops landed on the beaches of
Normandy in occupied France. The D-
Day landings were unexpected and the
casualties were lighter than the Allied
commanders anticipated. The Germans
attempted to surround the Allies near
the coast but after fierce fighting
American troops broke out of
Normandy in late July 1944. Germany
now faced a terrible war on two fronts.
Allied troops pushed the German Army
back, entering Paris in August 1944
and crossing into Germany in
February 1945. Two months later they
met advancing Russian troops on the
River Elbe. Germany finally
surrendered on 8 May 1945.

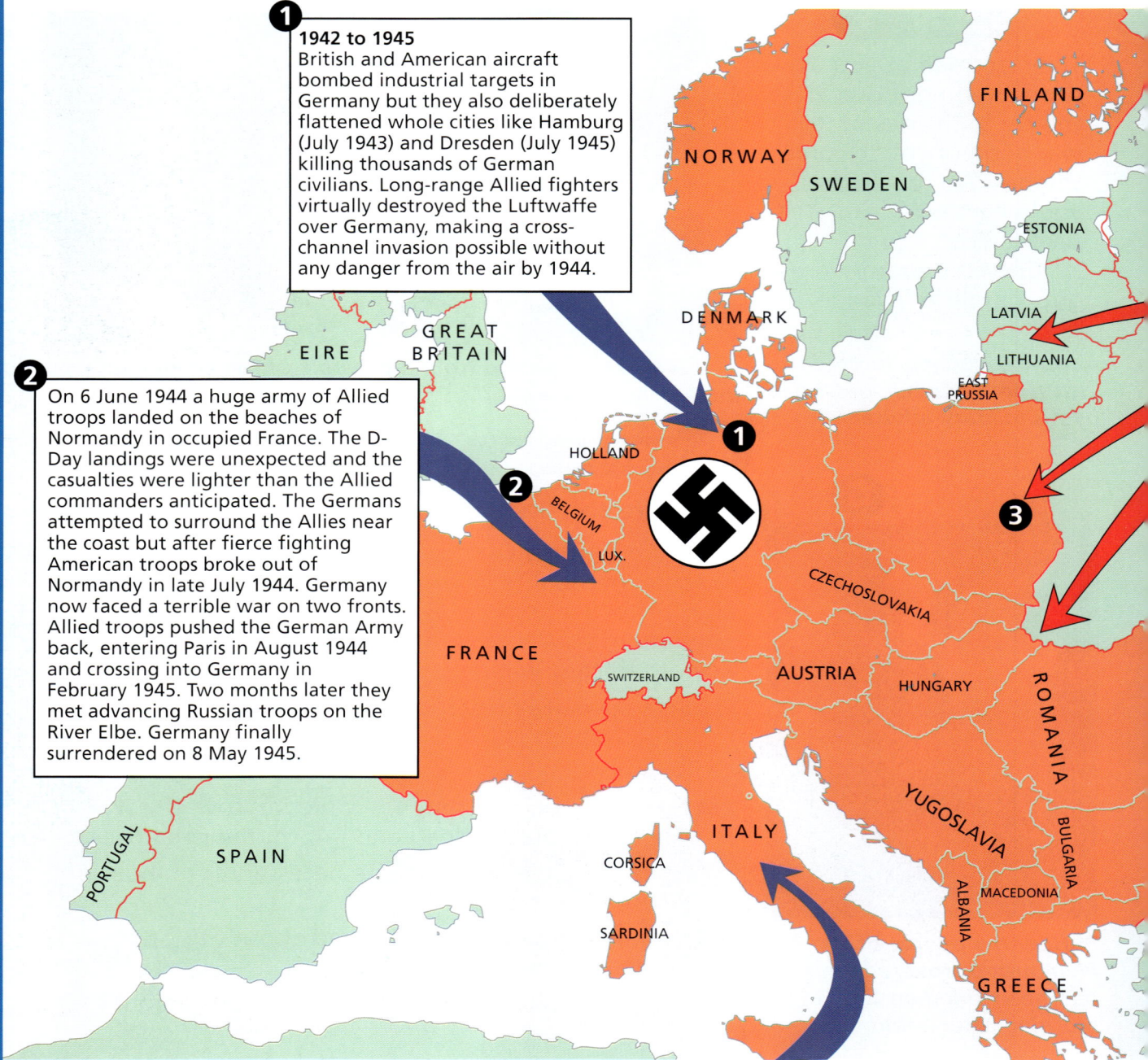

Q

1. Read pages 52–53 and 58–59. Draw a timeline from 1939 to 1945. Put the following places and events on your timeline. Explain what happened in each: Stalingrad; Battle of Britain; Dunkirk; the Blitz; Hamburg and Dresden; D-Day; Paris; Berlin; River Elbe.

2. Place an arrow at the point where you feel the war turned against Germany. Explain your decision.

3. Arrow the most decisive and the least decisive event. Explain the reasons for both your choices.

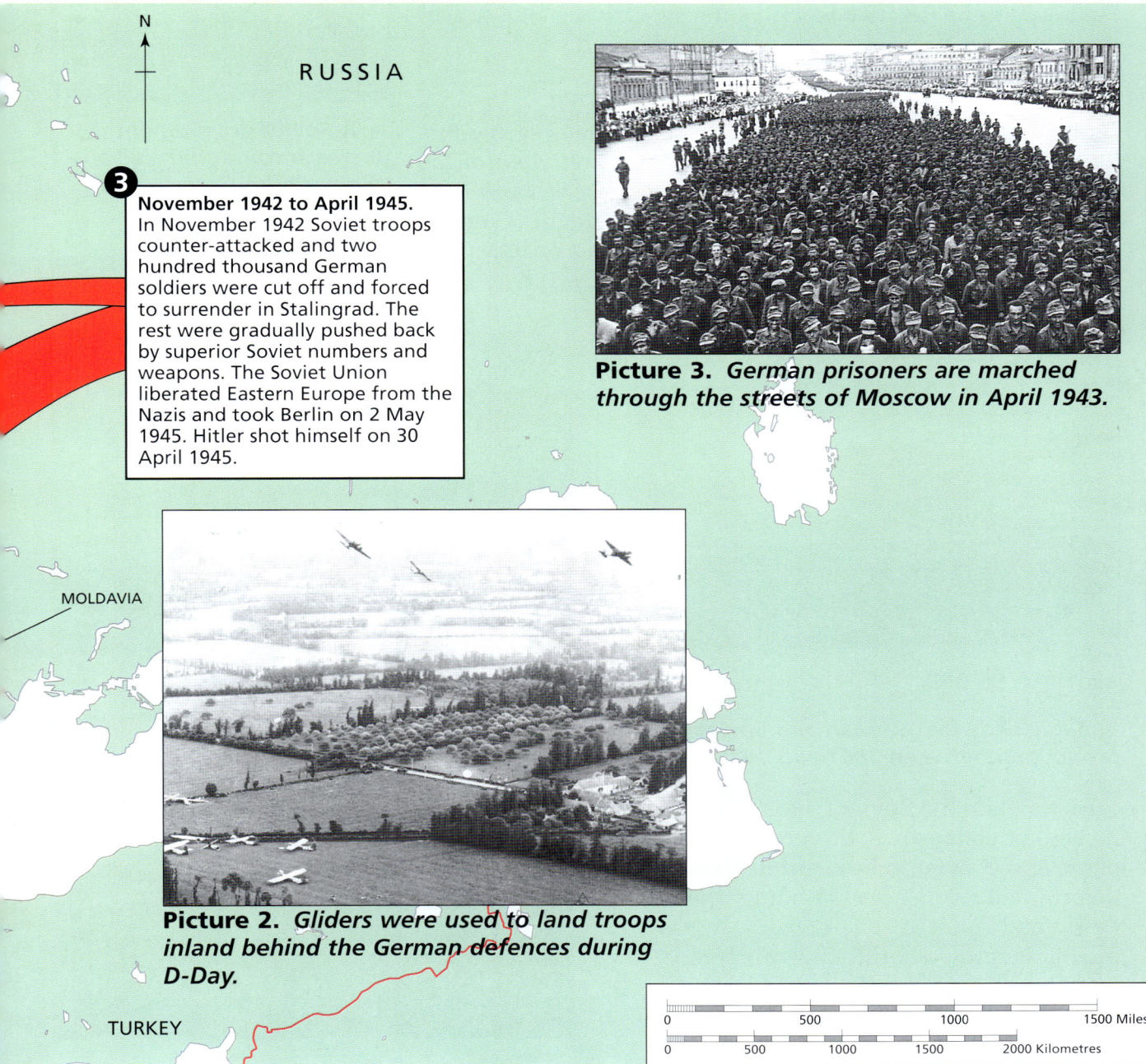

N

RUSSIA

3

November 1942 to April 1945.
In November 1942 Soviet troops counter-attacked and two hundred thousand German soldiers were cut off and forced to surrender in Stalingrad. The rest were gradually pushed back by superior Soviet numbers and weapons. The Soviet Union liberated Eastern Europe from the Nazis and took Berlin on 2 May 1945. Hitler shot himself on 30 April 1945.

Picture 3. *German prisoners are marched through the streets of Moscow in April 1943.*

MOLDAVIA

Picture 2. *Gliders were used to land troops inland behind the German defences during D-Day.*

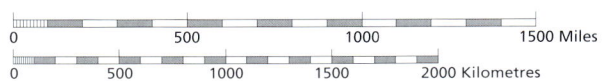

TURKEY

| 0 | 500 | 1000 | 1500 Miles |
| 0 | 500 | 1000 | 1500 | 2000 Kilometres |

The end of the Soviet Union?

KICKING IN THE DOOR

On 22 June 1941 Hitler launched Operation Barbarossa, a massive attack on the Soviet Union involving over three million men and four thousand tanks. He was so convinced that the weakness of communism and the racial superiority of Germans over Russians guaranteed success that he claimed 'we only have to kick in the door and the whole rotten structure will come crashing down'.

In the first few weeks of the attack it seemed that his prediction was coming true. The Red Army suffered a series of crushing defeats and many Soviet citizens actually welcomed the Nazis as a better alternative to Stalin's brutal brand of communism. Meanwhile the country was leaderless, Stalin spent the first two weeks of the attack lying on a couch in his country home in a state of depression and shock.

THE ATTACK STALLS

By the beginning of December 1941 the Germans seemed to be on the verge of victory, but they had not prepared for the terrible Russian winter which halted their vehicles and left many German soldiers to freeze or starve to death. Their harsh early treatment of Soviet civilians turned ordinary people against them and they were now harassed by thousands of angry resistance fighters.

SOURCE A

▲ **A Soviet government poster encouraging civilians to attack the German Army.**

A painting from 1948 showing Stalin personally planning a successful attack. ▼

SOURCE B

Soviets 95,099	Germans 53,800

▲ **Table showing German and Soviet tank production between 1941 and 1945.**

Meanwhile the Soviet Union was showing no sign of collapse. Stalin recovered from his panic and proved to be a ruthless and determined war leader. Although the Red Army had suffered severe losses, it was much bigger and could take much more punishment than Hitler realised. Many of its losses were replaced by the 1500 factories

SOURCE C

which were dismantled and moved further East by train. There they were out of reach of German bombers and could turn out huge quantities of weapons.

THE TIDE TURNS

In November 1942 the Red Army launched a huge counter-attack which cut off over 90,000 German troops at Stalingrad and forced them to surrender. A further German attack at Kursk was beaten off after a massive tank battle and from then on superior Soviet numbers and industrial production pushed the Germans back. In January 1944 the Red Army broke through to Leningrad and ended a siege which lasted 880 days and caused almost one million civilian deaths through starvation and enemy action.

THE END

By April 1945 over two and half million Soviet soldiers were poised just outside Berlin. Although their final attack was fiercely resisted by young boys of the Hitler Youth and men who were too old to be in the regular army, the city was forced to surrender. Hitler had spent the last few months in an underground bunker near the centre of Berlin. He shot himself on 30 April to avoid capture. A week later senior German officers arrived at allied headquarters to offer their unconditional surrender.

Hitler promoted his commander at Stalingrad to Field Marshal in the hope that he would be inspired to commit suicide rather than surrender! It didn't work.

Q

1. Why might **Source A** give an unreliable view of how Soviet citizens reacted to the Nazi invasion?

2. Look carefully at **Sources C** and **D**. How do they agree and disagree about Stalin as a war leader?

3. Which artist do you think is more likely to be giving his true opinion? Clue: Stalin died in 1953!

4. Which of the sources in this unit shows the most important reason for the Soviet victory over the Nazis? Explain your answer by describing the significance of each source.

SOURCE D

▲ *A painting from the 1980s entitled 'Stalin as War Leader'.*

D-Day

INVESTIGATION

THE D-DAY LANDINGS

The allied landing in Normandy was a great success. On all but one beach allied troops stormed ashore against limited resistance. The exception was code-named Omaha beach. American troops landing here encountered fierce opposition which cost them 2,400 lives. What was it like to be an American soldier leaving a landing craft and wading ashore into a storm of enemy fire? Read the sources below to find out.

STAGE ONE. *Waiting to go....*

Some people gambled, some read books, some prayed. We had a Catholic priest ... he held three services the night before we sailed, a Protestant, a Jewish and a Catholic one. I went to all three. He asked me what my religion was, and I said, 'whatever works'; that's the way I felt about it.

▲ *Lieutenant Bob Edlin. 2nd US Rangers*

STAGE TWO: *Nearing the shore*

Everyone was sea-sick ... the seas were six to eight feet high. By now most of the men were so sick they didn't care whether they lived or died. They were too sick to be scared. Even the sailors were sick. I steered the boat for five miles until they started to feel better.

▲ *Private William Ryan. 16th US Infantry.*

STAGE THREE. *Into the water*

When I stepped off the landing craft I was up to my neck in water. There were bullets pinging into the water all around me ... and then I got on to the beach and I lay there right next to my company commander. He looked at me and he said, 'What are you doing?' and I said, 'Same thing as you, sir.'

▲ *Private John Dandker. 16th US Infantry Regiment.*

▲ *From the film* Saving Private Ryan.

STAGE FOUR: *On the beach*

STAGE FIVE: *Getting beyond the beach ...*

STAGE SIX: *Afterwards*

It was now apparent that we were coming ashore in one of the carefully registered killing zones of German machine-guns and mortars. The havoc they had wrought was all around in an incredible chaos – bodies, weapons, boxes of demolitions, flame-throwers, reels of telephone wire, and personal equipment from socks to toilet articles …

▲ *Second Lieutenant Charles Cawton. 29th US Infantry.*

Eventually a US Navy destroyer came in as close to the beach as possible and started firing at all the German emplacements. In a little while two or three other destroyers started shelling as well.

▲ *Private William Ryan. 16th US Infantry.*

The only people on this beach are the dead and those who are going to die ... now get the hell out of here!

▲ *Colonel Taylor. 16th US Infantry.*

Our company commander was brought back and he had no legs ... and he just asked the doctor, who showed up from somewhere. 'I want to ask you a question, and I want you to tell me the truth. If I've got a chance I'll stay awake, I'll fight. If I haven't I'll go to sleep.' I often wondered if he made it ... I saw so many heroes that day, they just couldn't make enough medals for them.

▲ *John Hamilton. Radio Operator. 16th Infantry.*

INVESTIGATION

You are the investigator!

1. Describe how the soldiers' feelings changed at each stage of the landings?

2. Look carefully at both sources in **Stage Five**. What factors made it possible for the soldiers to get beyond the beach?

3. Do you believe that the officers at all times showed the courage and leadership which you would expect? Explain your answer by referring to **Stages Three**, **Five** and **Six**.

4. Imagine that you are going ashore with the soldiers in the **Stage Two** picture. Describe your landing on Omaha beach by taking the action through each of the stages shown here.

Remember, to do this activity properly you must provide a realistic account of the type of things which might have happened and how different soldiers might have reacted and felt.

11 THE FIRST NUCLEAR WAR

THIS CHAPTER ASKS
Why did Japan attack Pearl Harbor?
What was the War in the Pacific like?
Why did the USA use atomic weapons against Japan?

NEW WORDS

MARINES: Soldiers trained to fight from ships.
RADIATION SICKNESS: Illnesses brought on from exposure to the rays given out by a nuclear explosion.

An opinion poll taken in the USA during the war showed that one in eight Americans believed that all Japanese people should be killed.

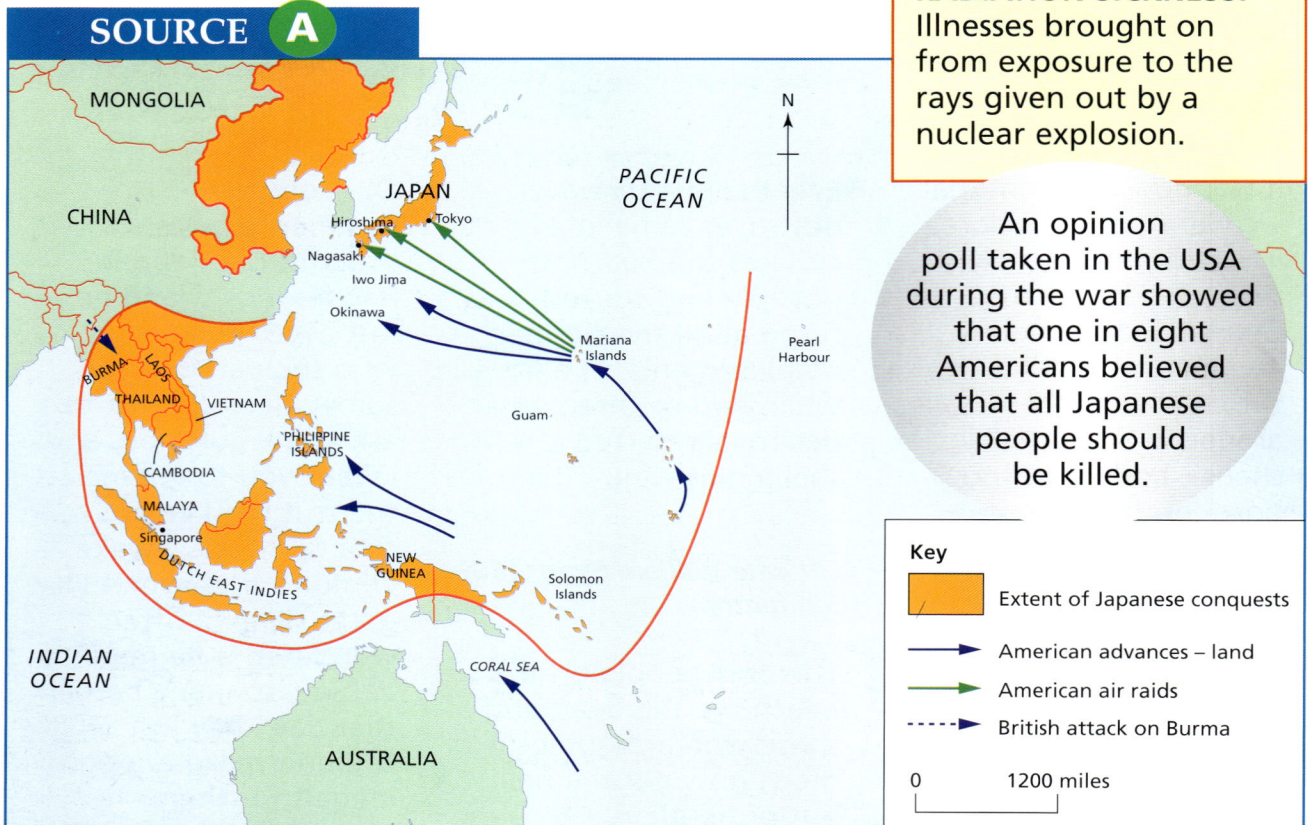

SOURCE A

MONGOLIA
CHINA
JAPAN
Hiroshima
Tokyo
Nagasaki
Iwo Jima
Okinawa
Mariana Islands
PACIFIC OCEAN
Pearl Harbour
Guam
BURMA
LAOS
THAILAND
VIETNAM
CAMBODIA
PHILIPPINE ISLANDS
MALAYA
Singapore
DUTCH EAST INDIES
NEW GUINEA
Solomon Islands
INDIAN OCEAN
CORAL SEA
AUSTRALIA
N

Key
Extent of Japanese conquests
American advances – land
American air raids
British attack on Burma
0   1200 miles

▲ *The war in the Pacific.*

JAPAN GOES TO WAR

During the 1930s Japan was hard hit by the depression and many Japanese looked to their armed forces for a solution.

On 7 December 1941 Japanese aircraft attacked the American naval base at Pearl Harbor in Hawaii. They hoped to paralyse the US Navy while their army overran the weakly defended European Empires in Asia. Within a year Japan had won a huge overseas empire but they had also enraged the USA, whose President Roosevelt vowed a terrible revenge.

THE USA FIGHTS BACK

The USA planned to take many of the Japanese-held islands and use them as a

SOURCE B

Each man should regard his trench as his grave ... it is your duty to kill ten of the enemy before dying.

▲ *An order to Japanese troops from General Kuribashi, commander on the island of Iwo Jimo.*

launch pad for an invasion of the Japanese mainland. The Japanese Navy was soon defeated but on the islands Japanese soldiers resisted fiercely, many preferring to fight to the death than suffer the dishonour of surrender. Although the USA was winning, their **marines**, whose job it was to take the islands, were paying a very heavy price.

THE BIG PICTURE

THE DEFEAT OF JAPAN

As more Japanese-held islands were captured, it became possible to bomb the Japanese mainland in preparation for an invasion which would end the war. From January 1945 American bombers rained down tons of bombs on Japanese cities, which burned out of control killing more than 300,000 people.

Instead of surrendering, however, the Japanese responded to the bombing with desperate measures, such as the creation of special suicide military units. President Truman became convinced that any invasion of the Japanese mainland would cost too many American lives. He sought a new way to make the Japanese surrender.

THE FIRST NUCLEAR WAR

Truman decided to use a new experimental weapon against Japan. On 6 August 1945 the first atomic bomb was dropped on the Japanese city of Hiroshima, followed three days later by another bomb on Nagasaki. The effect of the two bombs was devastating – perhaps as many as 120,000 people were incinerated by the heat and force of the blast, whilst up to half a million died later from **radiation sickness**. A day after Nagasaki, Japan surrendered.

SOURCE D

We seemed to possess a merciful short-cut to the slaughter in the East … to bring the war to an end and give peace to the world .. by a demonstration of overwhelming power at a cost of a few explosions.

▲ *British Prime Minister Winston Churchill's reaction when he heard about the atomic bomb.*

SOURCE C

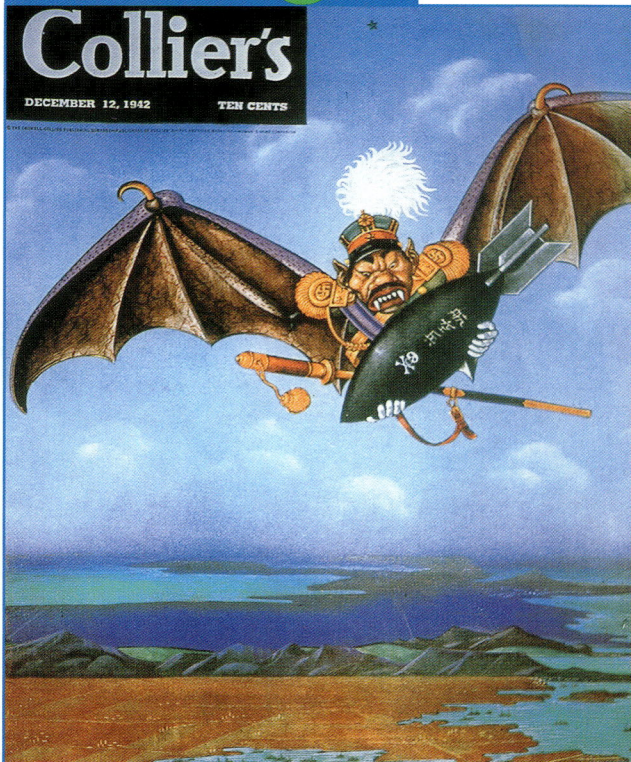

▲ *An American magazine illustration from 1942. What does it show about American attitudes to the Japanese?*

The most famous Japanese suicide units were the Kamikaze pilots who crashed their aeroplanes into American ships, but there were also suicide frogmen, sailors who sat on top of torpedoes and even men who piloted rocket-powered flying bombs.

Q How would President Truman justify using the atomic bomb on Japan? Probably he would refer to the following points.

■ How the war started
■ American attitudes to the Japanese
■ The failure of conventional bombing
■ The likely cost of an invasion.

Use these points to write a short radio broadcast to the American people on behalf of Truman justifying the use of atomic weapons against Japan.

Why did the USA drop the bomb?

YOUR MISSION: to discover the real reasons for the use of atomic weapons against Japan. Was it really necessary?

THE ARGUMENT

Since 1945 historians have argued over the real reasons why the USA used atomic weapons against Japan. Even today there are several different views. Your mission is to examine these views and ask, was the first use of atomic weapons necessary and justifiable?

SOURCE A

It was my reaction that the scientists and others wanted to make this test because of the vast sums of money that had been spent on the project.

▲ *Admiral Leahy, the American Chief of Staff explains why he thought the bombs were dropped on Japan.*

A US poster printed ▼ *during the war.*

SOURCE B

COUNTDOWN TO DESTRUCTION

1945

16 July
US scientists carry out first successful explosion in the New Mexico desert.

Mid-July
US intelligence intercept secret Japanese messages discussing possibility of surrender.

26 July
Allied leaders demand unconditional Japanese surrender.

28 July
Japan rejects allied demands for unconditional surrender.

6 August
Atomic bomb dropped on Hiroshima.

8 August
Soviet Union declares war on Japan and quickly defeats demoralised Japanese army in China.

9 August
Second atomic bomb dropped on Nagasaki.

14 August
Japanese representatives sign official surrender.

SOURCE C

All of us realised that the fighting would be fierce and the losses heavy. General Marshall told me it might cost half a million American lives.

⚠ **US President Truman writing about a possible invasion of Japan.**

SOURCE F

Everything became scarce. The food situation was gradually becoming worse and worse … even the army did not have enough to eat. With winter ahead, I said I cannot bear the responsibility for the lives of tens of millions of people dying a dog's death from hunger and exposure.

⚠ **Japan depended on the outside world for most of its food, but the US Navy had cut off all supplies. A senior Japanese government minister describes the situation in Japan in 1945.**

With his country in ruins and many thousands dead, the Japanese Emperor Hirohito used a radio broadcast to announce the surrender. He said, '... the war situation has developed not entirely to Japan's advantage …'!

SOURCE D

The USA was impatient to end the war before the Russians could effectively become involved and start making territorial and political demands in Asia.

⚠ **Roy Jenkins, from Truman, 1986.**

SOURCE E

It is His Majesty's heart's desire to see the swift end of the war … However as long as America and England insist on unconditional surrender our country has no alternative but to see it through in an all-out effort for the sake of the survival of our homeland.

⚠ **A private message from the Japanese government to its ambassador in Moscow. Japan might have surrendered but they wanted to make sure that their Emperor could keep his throne.**

SOURCE G

A demonstration of the new weapon might best be made before the eyes of representatives of all the United Nations on a desert or barren island.

⚠ **In June 1945 several of the scientists who helped to develop the bomb objected to its use against civilians. They suggested an alternative.**

❗NVESTIGATION

You are the investigator!

1. Sources A to D each give a different reason why the US might have used atomic weapons against Japan.

■ Explain each reason in your own words.

■ Put the reasons in order, placing what you think is the most justifiable first and the least justifiable last.

■ Do you think that any of these reasons really justify the use of atomic weapons against Japan?

2. Consider **Sources E**, **F** and **G**.

■ Do you think that Japan could have been made to surrender by more peaceful means?

12 THE NAZIS AND THE JEWS

THE BIG PICTURE

THIS CHAPTER ASKS

How did the Nazis treat the Jews?
Did ordinary Germans know about the 'Final Solution'?

NEW WORDS

BOYCOTT: refusing to deal with someone as a protest.

FINAL SOLUTION: the Nazi plan to murder all Jews.

MEDIA: newspapers, radio broadcasts and films.

SYNAGOGUE: a Jewish place of worship.

SOURCE A

◄ An illustration from a children's book showing Jewish children and teachers being thrown out of school.

HITLER AND THE JEWS

When Hitler came to power in 1933 there were about 600,000 Jews in Germany. Although they spoke German and generally mixed freely in German society, Hitler saw them as the distinct group which was responsible for Germany's problems. He blamed them for Germany's defeat in World War One and the economic problems which followed. He claimed that they were ruthless capitalists who exploited the working man but he also said that they were the leaders of world Communism!

Although many Germans may have disliked the Jews, few Nazis believed that attacking them was a top priority. Hitler was personally determined that the Jews must be punished. We may never really know why he hated the Jews so much. Some historians have argued that he had bad experiences with Jews as a young man, others simply think that he believed his own ridiculous claims about a Jewish conspiracy to destroy Germany.

EARLY ATTACKS ON THE JEWS

As soon as Hitler came to power he ordered that all Jews in the civil service and the law must be removed from their jobs. He also made sure that Jews were sacked from radio and theatre. Meanwhile a huge propaganda campaign was started to convince non-Jewish Germans of the threat posed by their Jewish neighbours. Newspapers made up false stories about the behaviour of the Jews and radio and films spread a message of hatred. Soon Jewish people were being casually attacked and insulted in the streets and the police refused to do anything to protect them.

THE ATTACKS GET WORSE

In 1935 Hitler introduced the Nuremburg Laws which gravely restricted Jewish rights. Later many of these laws were extended to keep Jews out of public places like parks and beaches and the Nazis demanded that all non-Jews should boycott Jewish shops.

In 1938, when an angry young Jew assassinated a German official in Paris, the Nazis **media** demanded a wave of attacks on the Jews across Germany. Mobs led by SS men and armed with sticks and hammers smashed and burned Jewish shops, homes and synagogues. Over one hundred Jews were beaten to death and perhaps as many as 30,000 others were taken off to concentration camps without trial. When the mobs had finished, so much broken glass lay on the streets that the event became known as *Kristallnacht* – 'glass night'.

Hitler's intention may have been to simply harass the Jews until they left Germany, but because they were not allowed to take any of their wealth with them, many Jews decided to stay in the hope that things would eventually get better. Around 30% of all Jews left Germany before the war but many were forced to stay because countries like Britain and the USA often refused to allow them in.

SOURCE B

A Jew cannot be a German citizen and cannot vote. He may not hold public office. Marriages between Jews and German citizens are forbidden.

▲ *Part of the Nuremberg Laws.*

SOURCE C

▲ *Jews are forced to scrub pavements in Vienna in 1938.*

Q

1. Make a list of the ways in which the Nazis victimised Jews. All the Nazi actions were wrong, some were worse than others. Start your list with the worst one.

2. You are a Jew wanting to leave Germany for the USA. But the USA refuses to allow you in. Use the sources to write an appeal to the American President explaining why you have to leave. Use the list you have written for Question 1.

Discussion Point

Which groups face discrimination in the world today? What should be done to stop this?

Was the 'Final Solution' a secret?

DECIDING ON THE 'FINAL SOLUTION'

After the conquest of Poland in 1939 and the attack on the Soviet Union two years later, the Nazis occupied large areas inhabited by millions of Jews. Orders were given for a 'Final Solution' in which all Jews were to be murdered. The first to be killed on a large scale were the Polish and Russian Jews. They were usually taken to an out of the way place and made to dig their own graves before being shot by firing squad. Hundreds of thousands of men, women and children were killed in this way, but it was not enough for the Nazis, a new system had to be found to make the killing quicker and more efficient.

THE DEATH CAMPS

From July 1941 onwards thousands of Jews from all over Europe were transported by train to huge concentration camps in the East. Many of these camps became factories for killing people and disposing of their bodies. Some victims died through the casual brutality of the guards; others were shot, beaten, injected with poison or used for deadly medical experiments. The majority were gassed.

INTO THE GAS CHAMBERS

Before being transported the victims were usually told that they were being sent away to work, but by the time they arrived at the camp they were usually too hungry, tired and afraid to care what happened to them. They were told to strip for a shower and then crowded into a large chamber. The doors were locked and the chamber would fill with poison gas for perhaps fifteen minutes. The bodies would then be carried out, but this was not the end. The Nazis were determined to get the maximum use of the corpses. They were boiled for soap, the bones were used for fertilizer, the hair for mattress stuffing and even the gold fillings in teeth were pulled out and melted down.

SOURCE A

If the Jews succeed in plunging the nations into world war the result will not be a victory for them, it will be the annihilation of the Jewish race in Europe.

▲ Hitler may have intended to murder the Jews all along. This is what he said in 1939, before the start of the war.

SOURCE B

▲ A scene at Belsen concentration camp when it was taken by Allied troops in 1945.

SOURCE C

… several times a week buses arrive in Hadamar with a considerable number of such victims. School children of the area know this vehicle and say 'Here comes the murder box again.'

▲ In 1939 Hitler gave orders for the murder of all mentally disabled Germans. They were the first victims to be murdered by gas. Two years later a German Bishop complained.

WAS THE 'FINAL SOLUTION' A SECRET?

The Nazis went to great lengths to keep the Death Camps secret and after the war many Germans claimed that they did not realise what was happening to the Jews. Yet it seems impossible that six million people could completely disappear without anyone suspecting that they were being murdered.

Ordinary Germans witnessed the transportation of Jews which was often timetabled and supervised by civil servants and policemen. Respectable German companies took orders for the poison gas for the murders and the ovens which were used to destroy many of the bodies. German and Swiss banks helped the Nazis to empty millions of marks from the victims' bank accounts and may even have helped to reprocess the gold from dental fillings.

THE RECKONING

After the war the leading Nazis were brought to trial at Nuremberg and many of them were executed. Many less important Nazis went unpunished and as late as the 1990s relatives were still trying to force Swiss banks to return money taken from Jewish victims. In 1999 perhaps the last of the accused was brought to trial in Britain.

SOURCE D

It was most important that the whole process of arriving and undressing should take place in an atmosphere of the greatest possible calm. People reluctant to take off their clothes had to be helped by those of their companions who had already undressed … the smaller children usually cried because of the strangeness of being undressed in this fashion, but when their mothers or the Jewish prison workers comforted them, they became calm and entered the gas chambers, playing or joking with one another and carrying their toys.

▲ *Rudolf Hess, Commander of the Auschwitz Death Camp, describes how Jewish prison workers were used to trick the victims into the gas chambers.*

SOURCE E

▲ *Allied troops force a German civilian to walk around a liberated Death Camp.*

Q

1. There is no definite evidence that Hitler ordered the Final Solution. How could a historian use **Source A** to show that Hitler was personally responsible?

2. Why did the allied soldiers force the girl in **Source E** to visit the Camp? Why was the picture taken?

3. 'Ordinary Germans must have known about the "Final Solution".' Do you agree?

Make a list of all the non-Nazi Germans who you think should have known. For each one explain why you think they would have known.

13 END OF EMPIRE

THE BIG PICTURE

THIS CHAPTER ASKS
Why did the Europeans give up their empires?
What problems did the newly independent countries face?

NEW WORDS
APARTHEID: a policy of keeping blacks and whites separate in South Africa.

INDO-CHINA: modern day Vietnam, Laos and Cambodia.

SOURCE A

Key
- Portuguese
- British
- British Mandate
- French
- French Mandate
- Belgian
- Belgian Mandate
- Spanish
- Italian

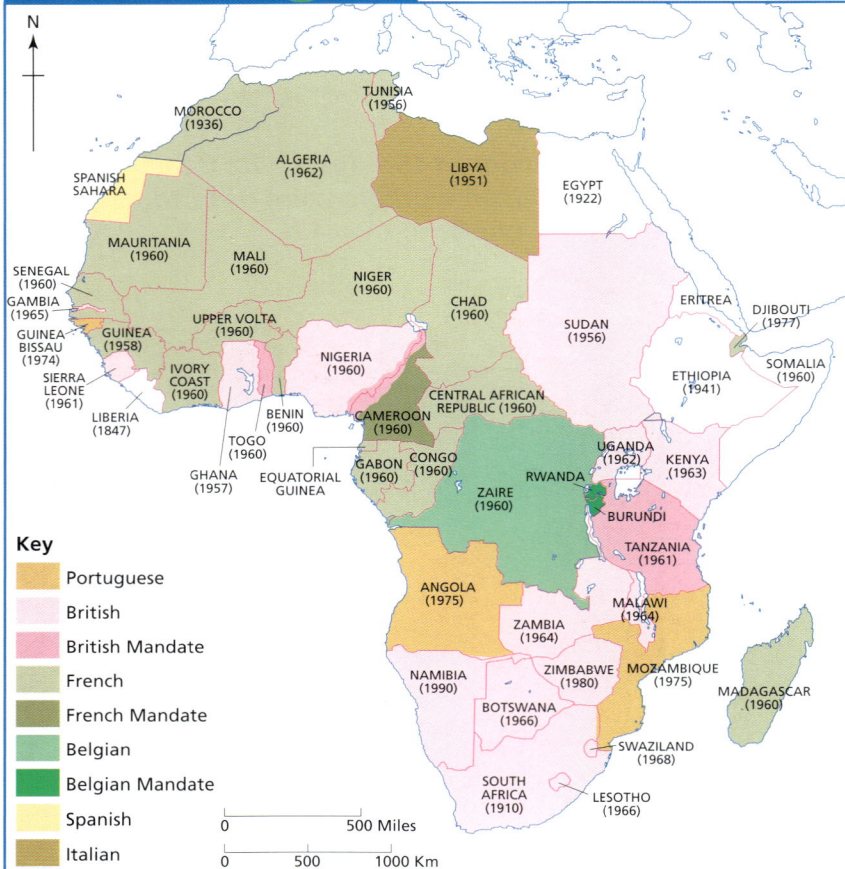

Of a total of 54 countries, 11 have had civil wars since independence, 32 have had military take-overs and only two have remained as democracies for the entire period.

◄ *Map showing African countries and the date of their independence.*

WHY DID THE EMPIRES END?
After World War Two, the European Empires gradually broke up into a large number of independent states. The war had changed attitudes. In Europe many people who had fought for their own freedom felt that empires could no longer be justified. In the colonies a number of European-educated Africans and Asians who had helped in the war against the Nazis and the Japanese now felt that they had a right to freedom for their own countries.

India and Pakistan were the first to gain independence in 1947, but in the next twenty years they were followed by many other African and Asian states. Usually this was a peaceful process because the Europeans were so weakened by the war that they wanted to avoid a struggle. Where they refused to go, however, there was violence. France fought two very bloody and unsuccessful wars during the 1950s in **Indo-China** and Algeria. These conflicts probably encouraged other European states to leave their own empires before they too had to fight expensive wars.

PROBLEMS FOR THE NEW COUNTRIES

Independence from Europe made the people in the ex-colonies very happy, but it did not solve all their problems. The greatest of these was poverty. Many of the colonies had developed industry and farming simply to supply their European master country, but with independence they found it very difficult to change their economies to provide for themselves. This problem was made worse by the richer states who did little to help their former colonies after independence. Most terrible of all was the problem of war.

CONFLICT IN THE NEW COUNTRIES

The borders of the new states were originally drawn up by Europeans without regard to who lived there. As a result, when these states were declared independent they often contained many people from different tribes and religions who felt that they had little in common and could not trust each other. These divisions often led to civil war, and from the chaos of war and economic problems, army leaders sometimes seized power from the elected civilian government. In many countries army generals set up brutal dictatorships which denied the people their freedom. In others, a single party took power and outlawed all democratic opposition.

Over one billion people around the world do not have enough food to eat and most of these are in former European colonies. In the 1990s, 24 people were dying every minute as a result of hunger; 18 of these were children.

SOURCE B

Saudi Arabia 2.7
Norway 1.1
Sweden 0.9
France 0.8
Belgium 0.4
Britain 0.3

▲ *Amount of economic aid given by richer countries in the 1990s expressed as a percentage of national income. The United Nations recommends a figure of 0.7%. Former imperial powers are shown in bold.*

SOURCE C

▲ *A teenage boy fighting in a civil war in Liberia in 1996. Children are often forced to fight in African wars.*

Q 1. Why were European countries usually willing to give up their empires? Mention the following:

■ World War Two
■ Changing attitudes in Europe
■ Changing attitudes in the colonies
■ Threat of violence.

Discussion Point

Should rich countries try to end inequality in the world today?

The end of apartheid

FROM PRISONER TO PRESIDENT

On the afternoon of 11 February 1991, a billion television viewers across the world watched pictures of a man being released from a South African prison. The man was Nelson Mandela and he had spent 27 years in prison for opposing the South African government. Incredibly, within four years of his release, he became the President of South Africa.

▲ *Nelson Mandela before imprisonment in 1960, and after his release in 1991.*

Nelson Mandela born 1918

The son of a chief who became a solicitor. He supported peaceful protest until 1961 when he formed a group which set out to destroy property without taking life.
Imprisoned in 1962. He turned down many government offers for his release and became the symbol of defiance to apartheid.

SOURCE A

… we felt that without sabotage there would be no way open to the African people to succeed in their struggle against apartheid. All lawful means of expressing opposition had been closed by law and we were placed in a position in which we had either to accept a permanent state of inferiority, or defy the government. We chose to defy the government …

▲ *Mandela explains why he decided to destroy white government property. He made the decision in June 1961, after the police shot dead 69 peaceful protesters at Sharpeville township.*

SOUTH AFRICA AND APARTHEID

At the time of Mandela's arrest South Africa was ruled by a white minority who denied the black majority any say in how the country was run. The white government introduced **apartheid** (separateness) laws which said that blacks and whites should live entirely separate lives within South Africa.

Apartheid was really a way of ensuring that blacks were denied a share of the country's wealth. Although the blacks had their own 'homelands' to live in, these were always in the poorest areas and they only covered 14% of the country despite the fact that blacks actually made up 70% of the population. Many blacks worked in mines and factories in white areas, but they were forced to live in camps away from the prosperous white cities and they saw little of the profits they produced.

Under apartheid many things like swimming pools, beaches and buses were reserved solely for whites and the rules were strictly enforced. A black person could get five years in prison for sitting on a 'whites only' park bench.

STAMPING OUT PROTEST

The South African police were often ruthless in their dealings with black people. Every black person had to carry a pass book which said who they were and where they were meant to be. Failure to carry the passbook could result in a fine and probably a beating from the police who had the power to arrest anyone and hold them without trial. The police used beatings, torture and even murder against black opponents, and on several occasions they fired on peaceful protesters causing many black deaths.

▲ *Police disperse protesters with bullwhips during a demonstration in the 1970s.*

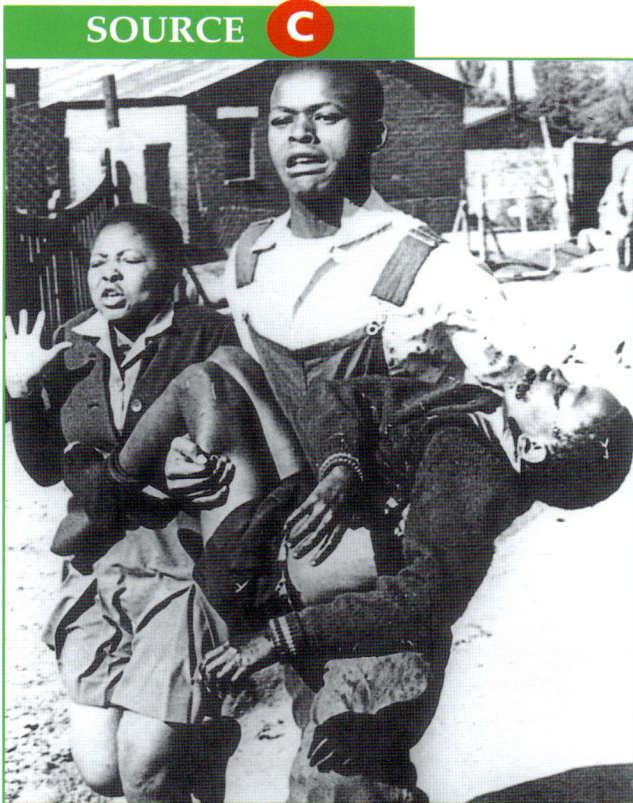

▲ *In 1976 the police fired on protesting students in the township of Soweto. Thirteen-year-old Hector Peterson was the first of 25 to be killed.*

THE END OF APARTHEID

Black Africans who wanted to resist the government joined an organisation called the African National Congress which dedicated itself to the end of Apartheid and equal rights for all. By the late 1980s South Africa was in deep trouble; the ANC was becoming ever more powerful and many of its younger members began to threaten greater violence. Meanwhile, other countries who didn't like apartheid and admired Mandela were refusing to trade with South Africa and this was causing severe damage to the economy.

Under pressure at home and abroad the South African government decided to release Mandela and negotiate with the black majority. A tense period of talks followed and, at times, civil war seemed a possibility. Once again, Mandela played a vital role by encouraging black people to be patient and seek a peaceful solution and in 1994, when the country finally held its first democratic elections, he became President.

Q **1.** Use the text and the sources to make a list of all the changes which you would like to see if you had been leader of South Africa during the apartheid years.

2. Use **Source A** to explain why Nelson Mandela turned to violence in 1961. Do you think he was right to do so? Support your answer with evidence from these pages.

14 WHO STARTED THE COLD WAR?

THIS CHAPTER ASKS

How did the Cold War start?

How close did the world come to a nuclear war by 1962?

What might have happened to ordinary people in a nuclear war?

NEW WORDS

ARSENAL: a store of weapons.

IRON CURTAIN: An imaginary line which divided Europe between the Communist East and the capitalist West.

THE WEST: USA and its European allies.

THE START OF THE COLD WAR

By the end of World War Two the Soviet Union and the USA were clearly so much more powerful than any other states that they became known as the Superpowers. They were close wartime allies against the Nazis but soon after the end of the war they began to quarrel.

They never actually went to war with each other, but for many years it seemed that they might at any time plunge the world into a Third World War. This period of tension is known as the Cold War. As you can see, the USA and the Soviet Union accused each other of starting the Cold War.

> The Soviet Union has been attacked twice from the West this century and we only took over Eastern Europe to prevent another attack. It is natural that we should want to protect ourselves by having friendly governments next door. The Soviet Union had no intention of threatening anyone.

> The USA deliberately threatened the Soviet Union with their atomic bombs. We were defenceless because we didn't have a bomb of our own. They spent huge amounts of money rebuilding Germany, probably so that the Germans could attack us once again.

> Truman was a hard, uncompromising man who hated Communism. He was to blame for the Cold War.

Joseph Stalin
Soviet Leader 1928–53.

Q **1.** Complete the following table using the text from the argument shown above.

Cause of Cold War	Why was it a cause?	Whose fault was it?	How do you think the problem could have been avoided?
Eastern Europe			
Military fear			
Germany			
Personalities of the leaders			

2. Who do you think was most responsible for the Cold War? Use your table to provide a detailed explanation of your choice.

3. Write a brief letter to Truman and Stalin making your suggestions for avoiding the Cold War.

After the war the Soviet Union forced many Eastern European countries to accept Communist governments who would be loyal to them. This showed that the Soviets intended to take over all of Europe and perhaps the whole world if the US did not stand up to them.

Most US soldiers were removed from Western Europe at the end of the war but Stalin continued to threaten the West by keeping the Red Army in Eastern Europe.

The USA had no choice but to help Germany; if we hadn't its people would have starved. Stalin was a brutal, untrustworthy dictator who had to be stopped.

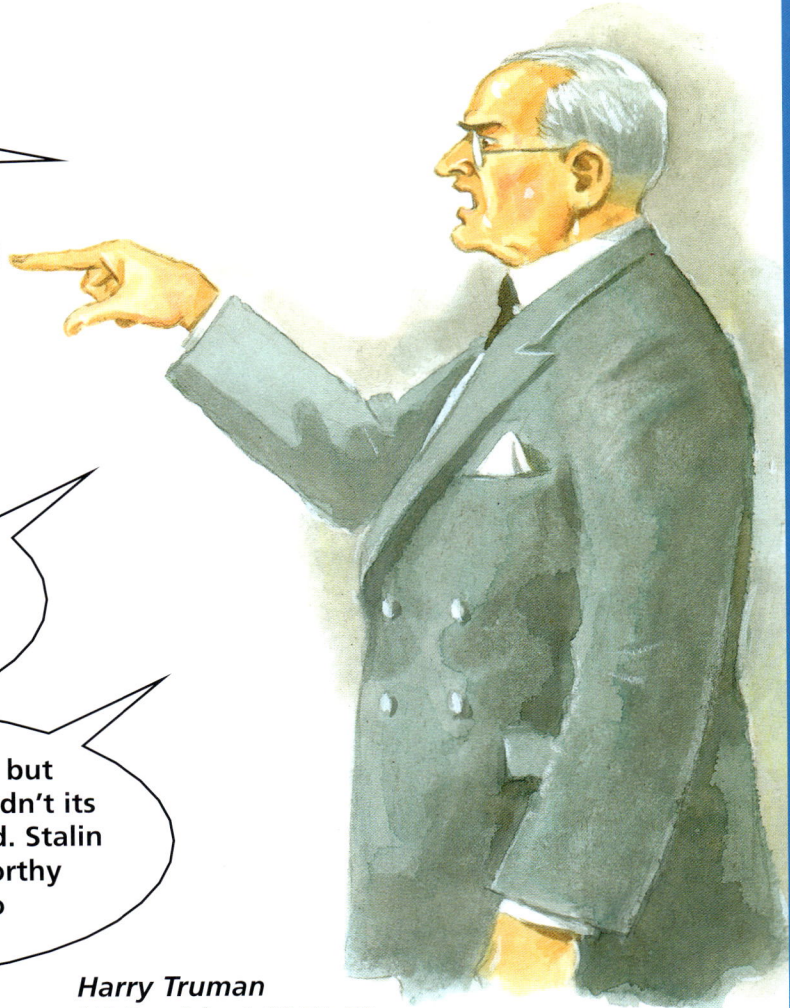

Harry Truman
US President 1945–52.

Almost World War Three?

HOW CLOSE DID WE COME?

The Cold War never did lead to a direct military conflict between the Superpowers, but war seemed close on several occasions. Both sides developed huge nuclear arsenals and new missile technology which could deliver destruction to anywhere in the world within minutes, so if there had been another war its results would have been truly terrible. Here are just three of the flash-points which might have led to such a Third World War.

Map of Europe in 1948. ➤

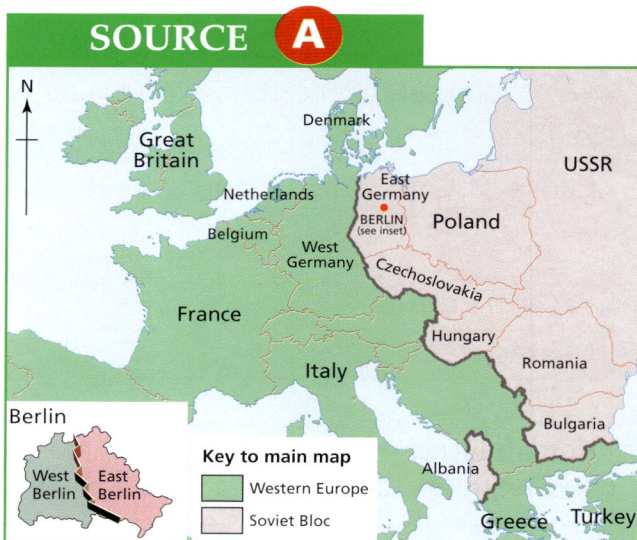

SOURCE **A**

Key to main map
- Western Europe
- Soviet Bloc

SOURCE **B**

◄ **In this Soviet cartoon the NATO states are shown goose-stepping like the Nazis.**

THE BERLIN CRISIS 1948–49

By 1948 Europe was divided between the supporters of the Soviet Union and the friends of the USA. The line between these two groups became known as the **Iron Curtain**. The only island beyond the curtain was West Berlin which was administered by the USA and its allies. Stalin was determined to remove the allies from West Berlin and he thought this could be achieved by cutting off all supplies from the East and blockading the land transport links with the West.

The West could not break through the land blockade without starting a war, so they supplied Berlin using fleets of aircraft. Stalin realised that if he shot the aircraft down it would lead to a war against the USA with its nuclear weapons, so he allowed the airlift to go ahead. By May 1949 it was clear that Berlin could not be starved, so the Russians gave up and lifted the blockade.

The West came out top in this crisis, but in late 1949 the Soviet Union tested its first nuclear weapon and there was no longer any guarantee that they would back down next time. Tension rose further because the Superpowers now formed their friends into two military alliances and soon the US-led NATO (North Atlantic Treaty Organisation) confronted the Soviet-dominated Warsaw Pact.

> Had there been a nuclear war in the 1960s, British defence planners estimated that Britain would have been hit with nuclear weapons as powerful as 20,000 Hiroshimas.

THE KOREAN WAR 1950–53

After World War Two, Korea was divided between the Soviet Union and the USA. Free elections were planned to reunite the country, but instead the Communist North invaded the South in 1950. China had already turned Communist and the USA feared that unless North Korea was stopped all of Asia might eventually be overrun.

The USA led a multi-national army against the North Koreans and soon pushed them back, but at this point Communist Chinese troops joined in the conflict. They were well supplied with Soviet-made weapons and soon the war became a bloody stalemate. Douglas MacArthur, a top US commander, was sacked for urging the use of nuclear weapons to end the war, instead, both sides eventually agreed to a cease-fire which left Korea divided.

CRISIS OVER CUBA 1962

In October 1962 an American spy plane spotted a Soviet nuclear missile base under construction on the island of Cuba. US President J.F. Kennedy realised that if the base were completed, it would allow the Soviet Union to strike at American targets without warning. He decided to blockade the island and he warned the Soviet leader, Khrushchev, that Soviet ships which were already on their way to Cuba carrying more missiles would be sunk if they attempted to break the blockade.

At first Khrushchev appeared willing to challenge the blockade and risk a likely nuclear war, but as the ships drew closer to Cuba he decided to back down and withdrew his missiles from the island. The Superpowers realised how close they had come to a nuclear war over Cuba and after this crisis they tried to reduce the risk by setting up a telephone hot-line so that, in future, both leaders could negotiate directly.

SOURCE C

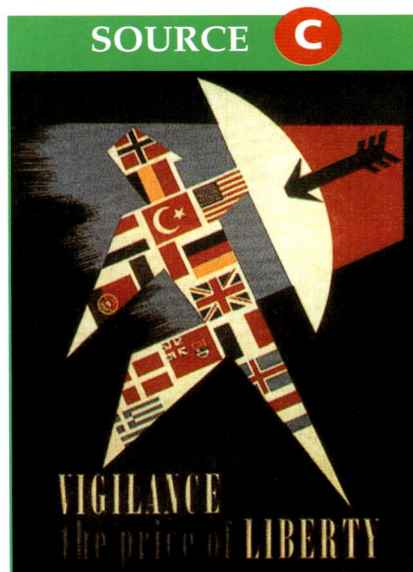

VIGILANCE the price of **LIBERTY**

▲ *A poster produced by NATO.*

SOURCE D

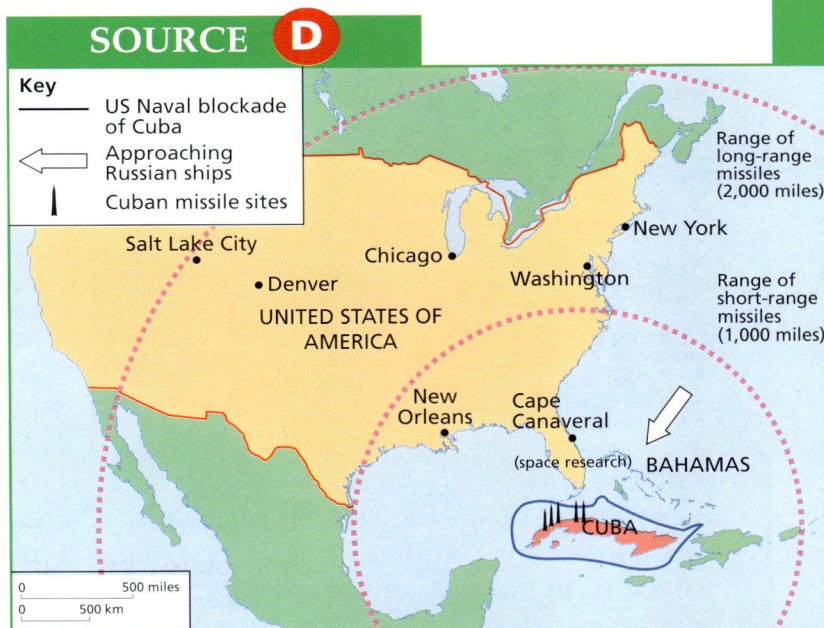

Key
— US Naval blockade of Cuba
⇐ Approaching Russian ships
| Cuban missile sites

Salt Lake City

Chicago • New York

• Denver Washington

UNITED STATES OF AMERICA

Range of long-range missiles (2,000 miles)

Range of short-range missiles (1,000 miles)

New Orleans Cape Canaveral

(space research) BAHAMAS

CUBA

0   500 miles
0   500 km

▲ *Map showing the range of missiles on Cuba.*

Q

1. How do **Sources A** and **D** help to explain the Superpower's disagreement about Berlin and Cuba?

2. How do **Sources B** and **C** disagree about the purpose of NATO?

3. Which crisis do you feel was most likely to lead to a nuclear war? Explain your decision.

4. Which crisis may have made an eventual nuclear war more likely and which one made it less likely? Explain your answer.

15 GLOBAL COLD WAR: 1960–80

THIS CHAPTER ASKS

How did the Cold War affect areas outside Europe?
Has the United Nations been a success?
Why did the USA lose the Vietnam War?

Q Explain how the global Cold War has contributed to the following:

- War
- Poverty
- The destruction of human rights
- The danger of a nuclear war.

THE SPREAD OF THE COLD WAR

NATO and the Warsaw Pact were too frightened of a nuclear war to challenge each other in Europe but after 1960 their struggle spread to other areas around the world with terrible consequences.

Central and South America

In some countries the USA tried to stop the spread of Communism by supporting anti-Communist dictators who took away political freedom and often tortured and murdered their own people. Communist terrorist groups also murdered their opponents.

▲ **Picture 1.** *Relatives of people who 'disappeared' in Chile protest in London, 1999. In some South American countries people were murdered by government thugs and their bodies were never found.*

Africa

In many of the newly independent African countries there were quarrels between the different tribes and political parties. Instead of helping to settle these disputes peacefully, the Superpowers attempted to gain influence by providing the warring groups with weapons and military advisers. Their involvement made African civil wars much more destructive.

▲ **Picture 2.** *Modern Soviet missiles on show in Ethiopia, one of the poorest countries in the world.*

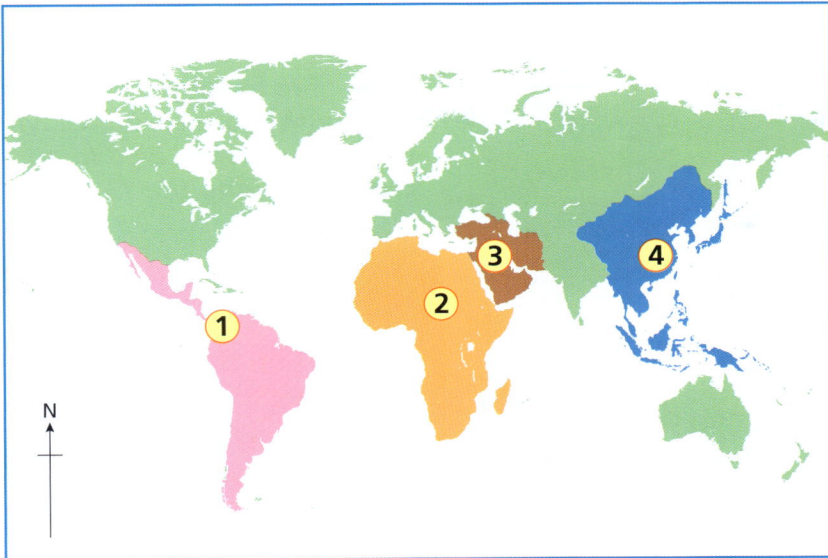

Q Use your findings and the photgraphs in this unit to produce a poster demanding an end to the Cold War. Your poster should show the effects of the Cold War on people around the world.

The Middle East

The USA supported the Jewish state of Israel. This meant that the Soviet Union was able to gain influence in Arab states like Egypt, Syria and Iraq who hated Israel. Both the Arabs and the Jews were heavily armed with the latest superpower conventional weapons. When Israel and the Arab countries fought in 1973 there was a real danger that both Superpowers might be drawn in.

▲ **Picture 3:** *The Iraqi supergun, possibly designed to fire nuclear weapons at Israel. Both the Jews and the Arabs have attempted to build their own nuclear weapons. It is likely that Israel succeeded.*

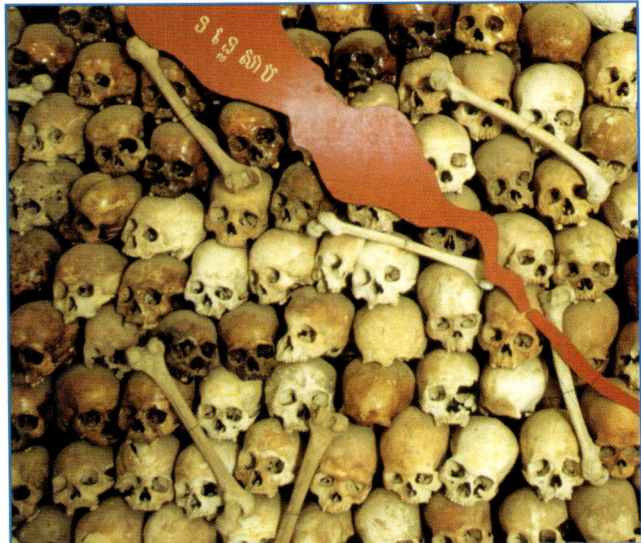

The Far East

The United States feared that Russia and China would try to spread Communism throughout this area. The Communists were stopped in Korea but the US army suffered a costly defeat in Vietnam. In other countries the US supported anti-Communist regimes. In Cambodia, China supported a brutal Communist government known as the Khmer Rouge, which murdered 1.7 million of its own people.

▲ **Picture 4.** *Skulls of many of the victims of the Khmer Rouge.*

The United Nations: success or failure?

◄ *United Nations armoured vehicles shelter people from sniper fire as they cross a road in the former Yugoslavia where thousands died in a civil war during the 1990s.*

In the 50 years after 1945 there were around 300 wars. In 1993 the UN had 60,000 peacekeepers in 14 different countries costing two billion pounds a year.

THE ORIGINS OF THE UNITED NATIONS

On 26 June 1945 representatives from 50 different countries signed an agreement called the Charter of the United Nations. Their aim was to set up an international organisation which would preserve world peace and solve problems like famine and disease.

KEEPING THE PEACE

The job of keeping the peace was the responsibility of the United Nations Security Council, but this body was dominated by the most powerful countries who kept a veto and were able to block any decision which went against them. This has effectively limited the peace-keeping role of the United Nations to disputes between smaller states. In a major crisis like Berlin or Cuba, the Superpowers simply ignored the United Nations and negotiated directly with each other. Even in disputes between smaller countries, the Superpowers have often taken different sides.

SUCCESSES FOR THE SECURITY COUNCIL?

The United Nations has managed to keep the peace in a number of areas around the world. Its blue helmeted soldiers with their white vehicles now separate fighting people in places like Cyprus and the former Yugoslavia, but this is generally only possible where both sides already want to stop fighting. The original aim of stopping wars from ever taking place is far from being achieved.

On the few occasions where the United Nations has taken action to stop war and punish an attacker, such as North Korea in 1950 or Iraq in 1991, it has been accused of simply carrying out the wishes of the USA and its actions have not met with the approval of Russia. In 1999, when NATO attacked Serbia, it simply ignored the UN because Russia opposed the action.

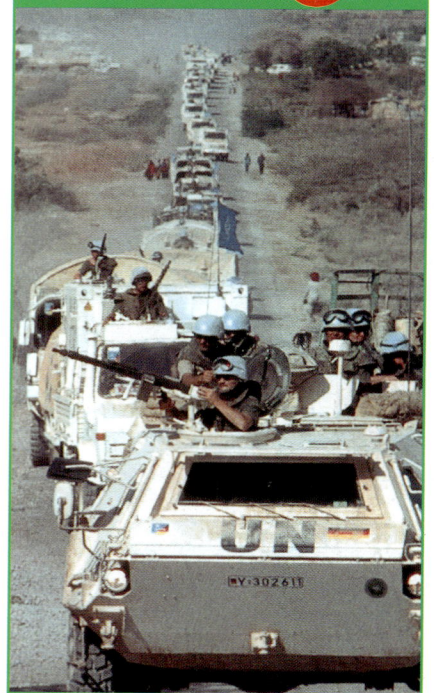

▲ *An UN food convoy forces its way through a war zone in Somalia, in 1994. Hundreds of thousands of Somalis were saved from starvation by such convoys.*

SOURCE C

Since 1950, life expectancy has advanced by almost 20 years and child mortality has fallen by two-thirds.

▲ *Excerpt from a United Nations report, 1985.*

OTHER SUCCESSES

Despite its poor record in maintaining world peace many other United Nations agencies have been successful. Health programmes have greatly improved the life chances of people in poorer countries, whilst educational work has increased literacy standards across the world. Other agencies have sought to improve agriculture and develop industry by providing loans and expertise where it is needed. This work has not solved the problems of world poverty and poor health, but it has helped to ease these problems.

DIVISIONS IN THE UNITED NATIONS

As more and more Third World countries gained independence after World War Two they were able to join the United Nations. For a while it seemed that their membership might lead to a fairer world as these countries pressed the richer nations to adopt policies which would help them. By the 1980s, however, it was clear that the wealthier nations would not support policies which improved the Third World at their own expense. Both the USA and Britain withdrew from the United Nations education programme because they thought it had become the political tool of the poor countries and the Americans actually went so far as to withhold part of their donations which help the organisation to survive.

SOURCE D

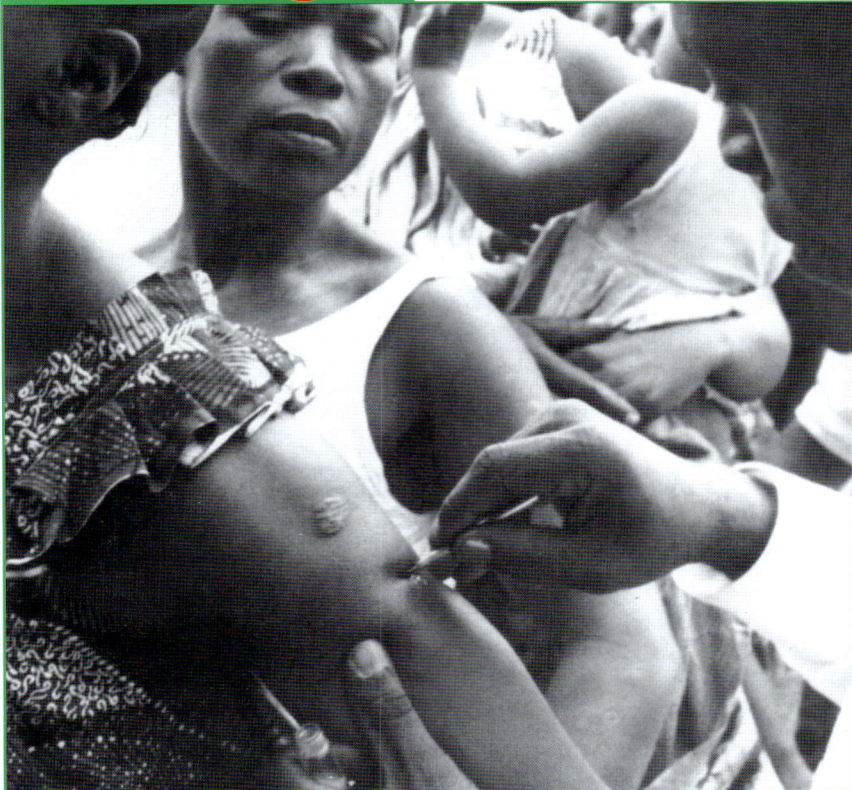

◄ *A United Nations doctor inoculates women in the Congo in 1960. Thanks to the UN the effects of many killer diseases have been greatly reduced and smallpox has been eradicated altogether.*

Q

1. Are **Sources A** and **B** evidence of the success or failure of the UN? Explain your answer.

2. Explain how its own divisions have made it difficult for the UN to maintain world peace and improve the lives of people in poorer countries.

3. Which of these two aims has the UN come closest to achieving?

Why did the US lose the Vietnam War?

INVESTIGATION

YOUR MISSION: to discover why the war in Vietnam became so unpopular with the American people.

NEW WORDS

CONSCRIPTION: A law forcing people to join the army.
EMBASSY: Government offices in a foreign country.
GUERRILLA: A fighter who does not wear an army uniform. He ambushes the enemy then hides.

THE FIRST TELEVISION WAR

During the 1960s the USA sent troops to Vietnam where they fought a Communist **guerrilla** army known as the Vietcong. Their aim was to prevent the south of the country from being taken over by the Communists, but although they used massive force they were unable to defeat the Vietcong.

There were many reasons for the American defeat. Their troops were not used to fighting in the jungle conditions of Vietnam against an opponent who was skilful, determined and well-armed with Soviet and Chinese weapons. Added to this, the Vietcong had the support of many of the Vietnamese people and often hid amongst the ordinary villagers. The US tried to win the war through massive force whilst attempting to win ordinary Vietnamese over to their side. Neither policy was successful and Vietnamese came to hate the US even if they did not support the Communists. Most of all, the US lost the war because the American people demanded the withdrawal of their army even if it meant admitting defeat.

Did the American people give up because of what they saw on their televisions?

▲ A South Vietnamese officer shoots a Vietcong suspect. The Vietcong usually only came out to ambush their enemies at night. This frustrated the American soldiers who often resorted to torture or even murder when questioning suspects.

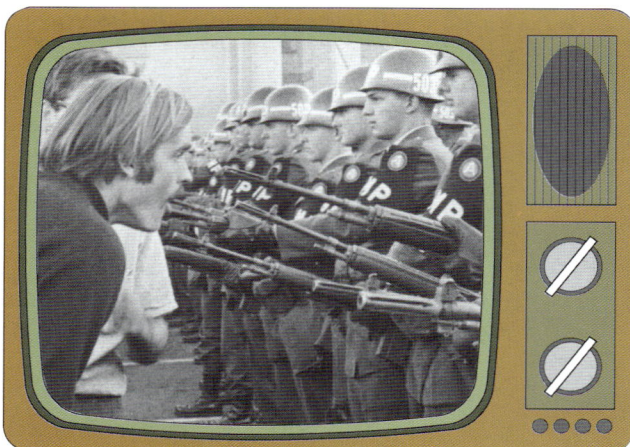

▲ Students protest against the war. Young American men were conscripted into the army and many were sent to Vietnam. Those who refused to go could be sent to prison, but many others burned their conscription papers and fled abroad.

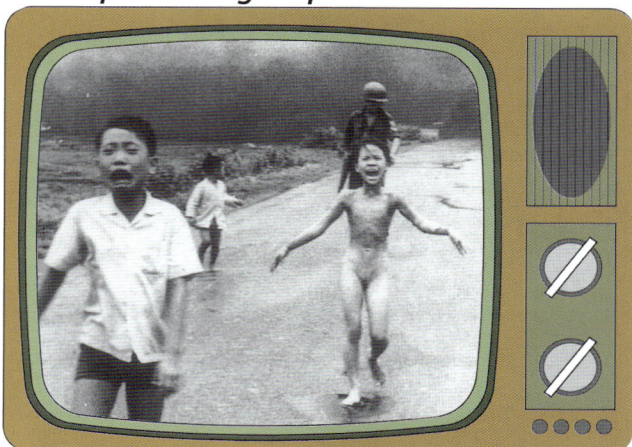

▲ A Vietnamese child burned by a napalm bomb. The Americans dropped more than seven million tons of bombs on Vietnam. They used napalm (a bomb filled with jellied petrol) to burn villages suspected of hiding Vietcong.

84

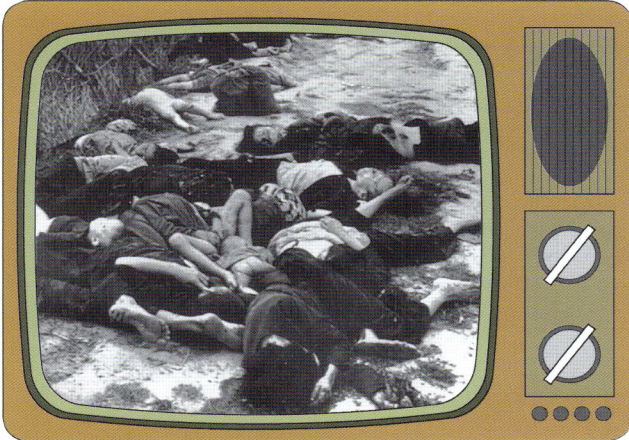

▲ *Murdered Vietnamese civilians in the village of Mai Lai. The US soldiers responsible were punished but over two million Vietnamese (10% of the population) were killed during the war.*

▲ *Dead American soldiers begin the long trip home. Over 50,000 US soldiers were killed in Vietnam.*

▲ *American city slums. The war was to cost $120 billion and this meant that plans to spend money helping the poorest Americans had to be abandoned.*

▲ *A dead Vietcong lying in the grounds of the US embassy in South Vietnam. By 1968 US commanders felt that they had nearly won, then the Vietcong launched the Tet Offensive. This involved attacking every major US base in Vietnam. Although the attacks were beaten off they convinced many Americans that the war could not be won.*

INVESTIGATION

You are the investigator!

You are the leader of a group of American students who are protesting against the war in Vietnam. After seeing these television images you decide to organise a protest march through your home town. Use the images to do three things:

1. Make up two anti-war slogans for the students to chant on the march. They must be less than ten words and they should rhyme.

2. Design your own protest poster for the placards which will be carried on the march.

3. Write a speech entitled 'We won't fight in Vietnam'. Include the following points:

■ The suffering of the Vietnamese people
■ The behaviour of US forces
■ The cost of the war to the USA
■ The inevitability of defeat

THIS CHAPTER ASKS
How did world Communism collapse?
Are people better off as a result of the end of Communism?

NEW WORDS

FREE ENTERPRISE: a capitalist system which allows people to use their money to set up their own businesses and make a profit for themselves.

GORBACHEV'S PROBLEMS

By the 1980s the Soviet Union was facing a severe economic crisis caused by the inefficiency of its factories and collective farms. The situation was made worse by the enormous cost of the nuclear arms race with the West. In 1985 a new Communist leader, named Mikhail Gorbachev, set out to solve these problems.

THE SOLUTION TO SOVIET PROBLEMS?

Gorbachev began by improving relations with the West so that he could reduce the amount spent on weapons. Then he introduced a programme of economic improvements which allowed greater **free enterprise**. His plans were fiercely opposed by other important Communists who feared that change would mean an end to the special privileges which they enjoyed as Communist Party members. Gorbachev decided to defeat opposition within his own party by allowing ordinary people from outside the Party to voice their criticisms of Communist rule. It soon became clear that most Soviet citizens wanted much more than economic change; they also demanded an end to Communism.

In August 1991 an attempt by leading Communists to overthrow Gorbachev was defeated when the army refused to deal with protesters who were determined to stop the old-style Communists from regaining their power. Within a few months the Communist Party was banned and new elections brought to power a non-Communist politician named Boris Yeltsin.

COMMUNISM IN EASTERN EUROPE

Communism was not an economic success in Eastern Europe either, but the people there knew that there was nothing they could do about it. They realised that if they tried to abandon Communism they would be invaded by the Soviet Union. In 1988 this situation completely changed when Gorbachev announced that he was beginning to pull the Red Army out of its bases in Eastern Europe and would do nothing to maintain Communist governments in the region.

Soviet workers often refused to work hard because of the low salaries they were paid. They said to their managers, 'You pretend to pay us and we will pretend to work'.

Q

1. Look carefully at all the information in this unit. What would you blame for the failure of Communism? Explain your answer.

2. Use the reasons below to explain why the Communist Party survived in China but lost power in the Soviet Union.

- Unity within the Communist Party
- The state of the economy
- Army loyalty.

Which factor do you think was the most important? Explain your choice.

WHY DID COMMUNISM FAIL?

◄ *Many workers quickly realised that they would get low wages no matter how hard they worked, so they became very lazy.*

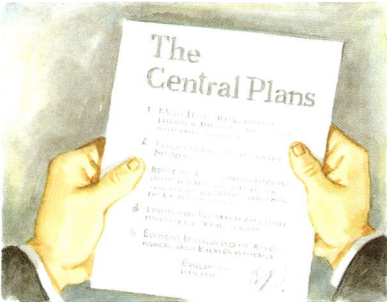

◄ *Local managers were not given the power to manage their own affairs. They were instructed by the central government who often had no idea of local conditions.*

◄ *The system soon became corrupt as leading Party members gained many privileges which they did not earn through work.*

◄ *Communism is really about sharing out existing wealth, but many of the countries which became Communist had been destroyed by war and were very poor in the first place.*

◄ *Communist countries always felt threatened by the West so they spent enormous sums of money on weapons which they could not really afford.*

The announcement led to a wave of uncontrollable protests all over Eastern Europe and one by one the Communist governments were forced to allow free elections and accept their loss of power to victorious non-Communist parties.

COMMUNISM IN CHINA

During the 1980s Chinese leaders abandoned their Communist principles and allowed many industries to adopt capitalist free enterprise. The changes soon made China one of the fastest-growing economies in the world. Western companies rushed in to take advantage of the cheap labour force available and the huge market for goods which China's massive population represented.

These changes, together with Gorbachev's reforms in the Soviet Union, led some Chinese people to hope that China would abandon Communism altogether and become a Western-style democracy. In 1989 student pro-democracy protesters gathered in Tiananmen Square in the capital Beijing. They soon discovered that the Government was willing to encourage economic reform, but would not release its total hold on political power. On 3 June the army moved into the square and slaughtered around 1,000 protesters.

The Berlin Wall

BUILDING THE WALL

In the early hours of the morning of 13 August 1961 thousands of East German workmen built a barbed wire fence all the way around West Berlin. In the next four days the barrier became a wall, and within a few years the wall was reinforced with a system of watchtowers and electric fences, guarded by dogs and by soldiers with orders to shoot to kill.

WHY WAS THE WALL BUILT?

Berlin was divided in two since the late 1940s. The east of the city was ruled by the Communist government of East Germany, but the west was part of capitalist West Germany even though it was almost one hundred miles away from the West German border. It was easy to cross the city from East to West and this made the Communists fear that West Berlin was being used as a stepping off point for spies entering Eastern Europe.

Much worse than the fear of spies was the fact that many East Germans were using West Berlin as a way of leaving the country. Western Europe was much more prosperous than the East and many people may have wanted to move to the West where they might have a much higher standard of living. They were prevented from doing so by the Iron Curtain, but during the 1950s around 250,000 people per year used Berlin as a way of leaving Communist Eastern Europe. They would simply cross into West Berlin and get an air ticket to Western Europe.

These people were often the youngest and most skilled workers who knew that they could enjoy a much higher standard of living in the West. By 1961 their migration was not only embarrassing for the Communists, it threatened to bankrupt East Germany by depriving it of its best workers. Meanwhile the West was able to use the people leaving Eastern Europe as evidence of the failure of Communism. Western leaders claimed that people were leaving not because they wanted a higher standard of living, but because they wanted the 'freedom' which Communism denied them. The Wall was built to end this embarrassment.

▲ *A West Berlin family waves across the wall to their relatives. Many families were split by the Wall.*

This young man was one of 86 people who were shot dead whilst trying to climb the Wall. Despite the guards many people did manage to escape. ➤

SOURCE **A**

SOURCE **B**

THE WALL COMES DOWN

With the end of Communism in many parts of Eastern Europe the Iron Curtain which divided the West from the East began to disintegrate. This made the Berlin Wall increasingly irrelevant since anyone who really wanted to leave East Germany could simply travel to other former Communist countries and cross into the West. The East German government could do nothing to end massive protests against them and, on 9 November 1989, they finally announced that anyone who wished could cross the Wall. There was a huge party and thousands of happy people headed for the West. Many of them joyfully attacked the Wall with hammers and attempted to tear it down.

AFTER THE WALL

Within a year free elections were held in East Germany and the Communists were heavily beaten. The Wall was torn down and, after more than forty years of division, Germany was united into one country.

The end of Communism and German unity did not solve all the problems as many people had hoped. East Germany was desperately poor. Its factories used out-of-date machinery, and much of its industry only survived because the Communist government had paid to keep it open. Western Germany was willing to invest huge sums in modernising the East, but it made no sense to keep many of the most unprofitable industries going. As a result many East Germans became unemployed. This created a great deal of anger and disappointment in the East, but the people of Western Germany were not happy either, many of them resented having to pay higher taxes to help the East. They came to view East Germans as lazy beggars.

SOURCE C

▲ A Berlin street party held on 10 November 1989 celebrating the fall of the Wall.

SOURCE D

Why do the Chinese smile? Because they still have a wall.

▲ A German joke from after the fall of the Wall.

After the fall of the Wall many police spies lost their jobs and became taxi drivers. A popular joke at the time said that when you caught a taxi you never had to tell the driver where you lived; he already knew!

Q

1. Explain why the young man in **Source B** might have tried to climb the Wall.

2. How do **Sources C** and **D** differ in their attitude to the Berlin Wall.

3. Why might East and West Berliners agree with the feelings expressed in **Source D**?

89

Is life better after Communism?

YOUR MISSION: to find out if the lives of ordinary people in the former Soviet Union have improved since the end of Communism.

THE GOOD NEWS

For many people the end of Communism was good news. They enjoyed much greater freedom from fear and for the first time they could vote in free elections. A sense of relief spread around the world as the tension and waste of the Cold War came to an end. Soon, however, ordinary Soviet people began to realise that Communism was not all bad and capitalism had its disadvantages.

1994 fighting breaks out in the former Soviet Republic of Chechnya....

1991 and a shale oil power station causes pollution.....

▲ The different peoples who made up the Soviet Union formed their own separate republics. Economic and political problems within these states meant that many governments soon started to take away political freedoms of their citizens.

▲ Large areas of Eastern Europe were polluted by heavy industry and unsafe nuclear power stations. The extent of the damage was only discovered after the end of Communist rule.

NEWS REVIEW ... NEWS REVIEW ...NEWS REVIEW ... NEWS REVIEW ...NEWS REVIEW ...

1994 a disabled man begs in a Moscow street....

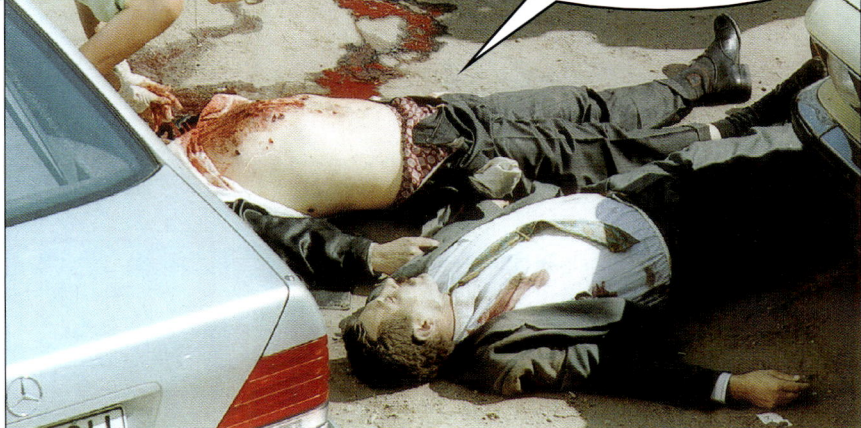

1997 the Russian mafia claim more victims ...

▲ *Without strict Communist policing, organised crime has grown powerful in Russia. Russian mafia members have grown rich through the drugs trade and many scandals suggest that they control important politicians.*

▲ *Under Communism there was always plenty of work and dependable pensions for the old, but the new governments had great difficulty changing to a capitalist system and soon many people found themselves unemployed and much worse off.*

1999 A child suffering from Aids in a Moscow hostel.

▲ *It is now much easier for foreigners to travel in Russia. This new freedom has led to the spread of infectious diseases which the government does not have the money to combat.*

INVESTIGATION

You are the investigator!

You are standing for election as a member of the new Russian Communist Party. Use the news items to write a speech criticising the government and describing why life was better under Communism. Finish your speech by explaining how you think Communists would solve the problems shown on this spread.

Discussion Point

Do you think Russia was better off *before*, or *after*, the collapse of Communism?

Have the challengers triumphed?

YOUR MISSION: to discover how the twentieth century changed the lives of some people.

CHALLENGERS AND CHANGES

The title of this book describes its purpose. During the twentieth century, the world has been changed by groups of people who were willing to challenge the existing situation in order to make their lives better and, in many cases, make the world a fairer place. In this unit are three images taken from news stories from the last few years of the century. You can compare them with the earlier images to show how much the world has changed, but some also hint at how much the world remains the same. Beside each picture is a reference to other pages in the book so that you can remind yourself of the situation earlier in the century. You can then answer the question, 'Have the challengers triumphed?'

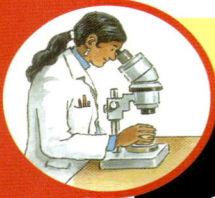

▲ Picture 1. Poster of black soldiers in WWI (page 48).

SOURCE A

▲ General Colin Powell. Top commander in the US Army. When he retired he considered running for President, but his family persuaded him not to because they were convinced that he would be assassinated.

◄ Picture 2. Photo of Nancy Astor (page 50).

SOURCE B

Women Labour MPs with ➤ Prime Minister Tony Blair after the 1997 General Election. In 1997, out of a total of 659 MPs, 120 were women. Women make up over half the population.